Quick Classroom Party Ideas

by Mary Anne Duggan

illustrated by Chris Nye

Senior Editor: Kristin Eclov
Editor: Christine Hood
Interior Design: Good Neighbor Press, Inc., Grand Junction, CO
Cover Illustration: Nancee McClure
Illustration: Chris Nye

© Fearon Teacher Aids

A Division of Frank Schaffer Publications, Inc.
23740 Hawthorne Boulevard
Torrance, CA 90505-5927

FE7956
ISBN 1-56417-971-0

Quick Classroom Party Ideas

Table of Contents

Quick Classroom Party Ideas

Quick Classroom Party Ideas

Introduction

What do you remember most from your early school years? Chances are, memories from special classroom celebrations are among the clearest. Long-term memories are created at classroom parties, making them excellent learning opportunities. Classroom parties can be more than just fun and games, however. *Quick Classroom Party Ideas* offers a wealth of entertaining, educational party ideas.

This resource features the following 16 parties:

Happy New School Year	Valentine's Day
Johnny Appleseed Day	100th Day of School
Grandparents' Day	Spring
Halloween	Earth Day
Thanksgiving	Cinco de Mayo
Winter	Mother's Day
Martin Luther King, Jr. Day	Father's Day
Groundhog Day	End of the School Year

Party ideas include:

decorations	activities
costumes	games
arts/crafts	recipes

Each idea has been classroom-tested and selected for its simplicity. The party suggestions also address the multiple intelligences, giving all learners an opportunity to be successful and enjoy the party.

Having party ideas at your fingertips takes away the stress of party planning. Take another stress-busting step by passing on this book to a parent helper to plan the party for you. With *Quick Classroom Party Ideas*, the party is already planned, leaving you the opportunity to enjoy special moments with your students and create your own memories that will last a lifetime.

Happy New School Year

- Balloon Desk Tags
- Party Favors
- Party Hats
- "Happy New School Year" Necklaces
- New Year's Nameplates
- Classroom Welcome Mat
- Class Quilt

- Balloon Messages
- New School Year Resolutions
- New Year's Countdown
- Time Capsule
- Auld Lang Syne
- "My New Friends at School" Book

- Class Secret Handshake
- Find a Friend
- We Have Hats in Common
- Noisemaker Fun
- Goose Hunt
- Chinese New Year
- "New Friends" Trail Mix
- Cool School Pops

Happy New School Year   Decorations

Balloon Desk Tags

For an eye-catching desk tag, inflate a balloon for each child. Write his or her name on the bottom. Tape the balloons to students' desks to serve as desk tags for the first day of school. Students can be grouped according to balloon color for later activities, or, use school colors as a springboard for patterning activities.

Party Favors

Make your classroom an inviting place by throwing a Happy New School Year Party! Students will be enticed into a classroom decorated with balloons, noisemakers, confetti, and streamers, all of which can be used for learning activities throughout the day.

Happy New School Year   Costume

Party Hats

Give each child a triangle of white construction paper. (Open a party hat to use as a pattern.) Supply each child with crayons, markers, sequins, confetti, feathers, and glue sticks for decorating their hats. When the triangles are dry, glue the side edges together to make hats. Punch a hole in two sides of each hat with a hole punch or scissors. Tie a 10" (25cm) piece of yarn to each hole. Tie yarn ends together under children's chins to fasten the hats.

"Happy New School Year Necklaces"

Students enjoy marching out with something special to show Mom or Dad after school. Use this pattern to make Happy New School Year necklaces. Poke two holes at the top and string with yarn. Students can color and decorate the necklaces any way they wish. For added fun, have students place the necklaces around their mom's, dad's or sitter's neck!

New Year's Nameplates

The balloon desk tags will only last a couple days, so have students make nameplates from 3" x 9" (7.5cm x 22.5cm) pieces of tagboard. Write or have your students write their names on the tagboard. Provide students with sequins, feathers, glitter glue, confetti, markers, and other art supplies to decorate their nameplates. These will last throughout the year and help students remember their wonderful first day of school.

Classroom Welcome Mat

Make your classroom "homey" by creating a classroom welcome mat. Find a carpet remnant, possibly one with finished edges. The more tightly woven the thread, the better. (Beware of remnants with stain-resistant coating.) Use tempera paint to write the word *welcome* on the mat. Place assorted colors of tempera paint in aluminum pie pans. Then have each student dip his or her hand in the paint and press it onto the mat. Depending upon the surface the mat is placed on, you may need to secure the mat to the floor with special tape. If the mat cannot be safely placed on the floor, it makes a cozy wall decoration as well.

Class Quilt

Another way to warm up your classroom is to make a class quilt. Punch holes 1/2" (1cm) apart around the perimeter of 8 1/2" (21cm) squares of white construction paper, one for each student. Students can decorate the squares with pictures or magazine cutouts which tell something about their interests, hobbies, preferences, family, and background. Each child's name should be prominently placed on his or her square for easy identification. Ask students not to cover up the pre-punched holes. Sew individual quilt squares together with yarn, and display the quilt on a classroom wall.

Balloon Messages

Copy and cut out the following questions and attach each to a separate balloon.

What is your favorite color?

Do you have any pets? What are they?

What did you eat for breakfast?

What is your favorite animal?

What do you like to do with your family?

Do you have any sisters?

What is your favorite food?

What did you do over the summer?

What do you want to learn how to do?

What is your favorite place in the world?

What do you collect?

What is your favorite song?

What is your favorite game?

Do you have any brothers?

How do you get to school?

What is your favorite book?

What is the name of one of your friends?

What is your favorite thing to do?

Are you the youngest, oldest, or middle child?

In what month is your birthday?

What is your favorite T.V. show?

What is your favorite sport?

What do you want to do when you grow up?

What is your favorite restaurant?

Who is your hero or heroine?

What color are your eyes?

Balloon Messages - continued

What is one thing you're really good at?

What is your favorite kind of weather?

How old are you?

What is your favorite movie?

These questions serve as springboards for discussions that help students get to know each other. Some questions are more difficult than others. Consider color-coding the balloons according to the difficulty level, and pass them out accordingly.

6   Reproducible

New School Year Resolutions

A resolution is a goal. Help students set goals for the new school year. Model goal-setting first, providing many examples for younger students. Have students write or dictate their goals on precut construction-paper balloon shapes. Mount the balloons on a bulletin board, or glue them on paper for a class book.

New Year's Countdown

What would a New Year's party be without a countdown? Practice counting down from ten throughout the day. Increase that number for older students. At the end of the day, count down the seconds before the bell rings. If your bell is unpredictable, create your own end of the school day. Arbitrarily choose a time for counting down, and finish with a rousing cheer of "Happy New School Year!"

Time Capsule

The beginning of the school year brings hopes and wishes for all that is to come. Invite students to put together a time capsule filled with their hopes and wishes for the new school year. Make a ceremony of "planting the seeds for a great school year." Dig up the time capsule on the last day of school.

Auld Lang Syne

Make this song, sung to the tune of "Auld Lang Syne," part of your closing for the first few days of school. Have students stand in a circle, cross their arms, and clasp hands.

A wonderful school day we've had,

And we'll have so many more.

The friends we've met, the fun we've shared,

And there's so much more in store.

For we're a classroom family,

Even though we've just begun.

We'll learn and change and grow each day,

While we laugh and have some fun!

"My New Friends at School" Book

Make a 6" x 9" (15cm x 22.5cm) booklet with four to eight pages and a front and back cover for each student. After students have had a chance to meet each other, send them around the classroom with their "My New Friends at School" books. Ask children to find a friend they'd like to meet, and ask that student to write his or her name on one page in the book. The student making the request then draws a picture of the new friend in his or her book. Parents will enjoy getting a first look at their child's new friends.

Class Secret Handshake

Help your students bond as a community by creating a secret handshake. The handshake can be simple or complex, depending on the level of your students. In order to give all children a "hand" in creating this shake, divide the class into small groups. Let each group devise a part of the handshake (e.g., one group thinks of incorporating a high-five, another suggests a little bump with the hips). Put all the pieces together for a fun classroom tradition.

9

Find a Friend

Ask students to stand in a circle and close their eyes. Take a variety of noisemakers and place one in each child's hand. Have students keep their eyes closed and make noise with their noisemakers, while listening for similar sounds from other noisemakers. Have students drift toward "like-sounding" noises until all children with similar noisemakers are all standing together.

We Have Hats in Common

Use the party hats students made to play this "getting-to-know-you" game. Have students put on their party hats and stand in a circle. Choose one student to stand inside the circle. That student is then blindfolded (or simply closes his or her eyes) and spins around while pointing one finger. Tell the student to stop, and remove the blindfold. The student to whom the child is pointing has to say one thing the two students' hats have in common (e.g., "They both have purple polka-dots." "They both have a blue feather."). Afterwards, that student goes to the center of the circle. Extend this game to include physical ("We both have brown hair!") and personality traits ("We both like to jump rope!") students have in common.

Noisemaker Fun

Another way to get students acquainted is to play a game of Noisemaker Fun. Give each child a noisemaker and ask a series of questions, such as "Who is new to our school?" and "Who had eggs for breakfast this morning?" Students who can answer "me" to any of the questions make noise with their noisemakers. Try to ask questions which only a few students can answer. Encourage students to not speak out, but to use their noisemakers to communicate. This is a great way to begin a discussion about the classroom procedure of raising hands to communicate.

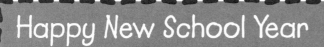

Goose Hunt

Introduce your students to the school campus with a Goose Hunt! Plant the clues on pages 11 and 12 around the school according to the picture in the upper right-hand corner. Place a stuffed animal at the end of the hunt along with a plate of cookies or some other treat. Use the stuffed animal as your take-home reading animal, which students will take turns taking home. Plant the first clue in your classroom and "discover" it at the right moment during your first day. Read the clue, and ask students if they would like to hunt for more clues. Clues can be modified or their order changed to fit your school's design.

Goose Hunt Clues

Classroom – You don't know me, not yet. But we'll be great friends, I'll bet. So follow some clues to find me. With the help of your teacher, together we'll soon be. But before I give you the first clue, there is something important you must do. Listen to your teacher explain the following procedures: the quiet signal, raising hands, and restroom and drink rules. Boys and girls, if you listen well, the first clue to you I will tell: I'm not known for my good looks, but find your next clue where you find lots of books. I forgot the most important direction of all – Walk calmly and quietly in the hall.

Library – Boys and girls, look, look! Everywhere you look is a book. We will come here each week, and into some books we'll take a peek. Let's go on another walk, but not for long.

Just go to the place where you can get strong (if going to the gymnasium). Or . . . just go to the place of music and song (if going to the music room).

Music Room or Gymnasium –

<u>Gymnasium:</u> The gymnasium! Wow! What a place! Plenty to do with plenty of space. One thing to remember, so you won't get the blues, on gym days remember to wear your gym shoes.

<u>Music Room:</u> The music room! Wow! What a place! You will sing many songs in this space. One thing to remember, so you won't sing the blues, if you sing with your heart you'll never lose.

The next clue will lead you to an area full of things—one of which you're sure to love, our famous playground swings.

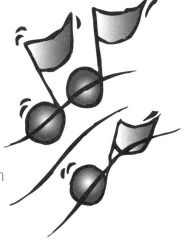

Goose Hunt Clues

Playground - Welcome to a place you'll be spending lots of time. Take a moment for a break. When the whistle blows, return for a rhyme.

Some of you have already noticed, and some of you have not. Here we have restrooms and a water fountain if you're hot.

Where would you go if you had an "owie"? Go there now, or I'll have a "cowie"!

Nurse's Office - Thank heavens for our school nurse. Listen carefully for another verse. There is one person at our school who is leader of us all. Find a person nearby, who is kind, nice, and tall.

Principal's Office - Our principal is a friend, dear and true. He or she will always be here to help you. Dearest friends, you have almost found me. Look for the food, and there I shall be. I can't wait to see you!

Cafeteria - At last we meet! Hello (teacher's name)'s clan. Now listen carefully to my great plan. Like some of you, I'm new to this school. I'm trying hard to learn every rule. There's one thing I want to learn how to do—to read books, and I need help from you. Please send me home with one person each day. Read to me at home. I'll learn to read this way. One more request, and we'll end this game. When you get back to the room, please give me a name.

Chinese New Year

On Chinese New Year, the Chinese add one year to their present age, no matter when they were born. For this game, have students sit in a circle on the floor. Give students a large ball to roll between them. When a student catches the ball, ask, "If this were Chinese New Year, how old would you be?" This way, you can assess students' abilities to solve problems involving addition. After the student gives an answer, say, "But it's not the Chinese New Year, so (child's name) must be (age)." You can then see how easily students can take one away from a number.

"New Friends" Trail Mix

Caution: Check for food allergies before students come to school on the first day. Peanuts can be life-threatening for students with peanut allergies.

Ingredients:

shelled peanuts   bite-sized crackers

small pretzels   goldfish crackers

sunflower seeds

Materials:

5 mixing bowls   paper cups

5 mixing spoons   sandwich bags

Have each student stand by the ingredient he or she is most like. Ask students to explain why (e.g., "I'm like a goldfish because I like to swim." "I'm like a pretzel because I like gymnastics." "I'm like a peanut because I'm nutty."). Allow each child to fill his or her cup with the chosen ingredient. Next, mix up the groups by having one person from each group stand by a bowl. Have the five students pour their different ingredients in the bowl and mix with the spoon. Each student can then fill a sandwich bag with trail mix and enjoy the snack with their new friends.

Cool School Pops

In some countries at New Year's time, red food is considered good luck. Your students will feel lucky making cool school pops to cool off with at the end of their first day. You'll need to start early in the day—the freezing time for cool school pops is at least three hours. To make cool school pops, you will need the following for every six children:

Ingredients:

16-oz. (500ml) package plain lowfat yogurt
10 strawberries
red food coloring

Materials:

blender
plastic knives
paper plates
6-oz. (187.5ml) Styrofoam cups
popsicle sticks

(cont'd)

Cool School Pops – continued

Have students cut the tops off the strawberries, using paper plates as cutting boards. Thoroughly rinse the strawberries, and cut them into small chunks. Blend yogurt, strawberry chunks, and a few drops of red food coloring in the blender. (Pops will come out pink.) Fill the Styrofoam cups halfway with the yogurt mixture and freeze for about two hours or until half frozen. Take cups out, put a popsicle stick in each, and return pops to the freezer. When frozen, remove pops from the cups and enjoy. If necessary, run cups under warm water to loosen the pops, or simply peel the cups away from the pops.

Johnny Appleseed Day

- Apple Teacher Items
- Cooking Pot Hats
- Apple Stamps
- Apple-Seed Pictures
- I Can Make a Difference

- Estimating and Counting Seeds
- An Apple for the Student
- Storytelling
- Johnny Appleseed Messages

- Cooking Pot Relay
- Squatter's Game
- Applesauce
- Dried Apples

Johnny Appleseed Day   Decorations

Apple Teacher Items

Johnny Appleseed is a folk hero whose real name was John Chapman. Born in 1774, Johnny Appleseed is famous for planting numerous apples trees from New England to the Ohio River Valley. The legend of Johnny Appleseed makes for good lessons on storytelling and legends, as well as altruism (Appleseed was said to be a friend to the poor). The legend is also a good introduction to discussions on environmental awareness. Johnny Appleseed was scoffed for his efforts to make the world a better place by planting his trees, but that didn't stop him from making a difference. This is a powerful lesson for students.

Apple items abound in teacher supply stores. Make a display of all those teacher gifts you've received that have apples on them. Set an apple on each student's desk to be used for Johnny Appleseed activities.

Cooking Pot Hats

For each hat, cut a gray or black strip of paper 9" (22.5cm) high, and long enough to go around students' heads. Glue or tape ends together to fit snuggly around each student's head. Trace the circumference of the hat on the same color paper and cut it out. Tape the circle to the strip to make the bottom of the pot. Make a handle for the pot by folding a 9" x 12" (22.5cm x 30cm) piece of black paper in half lengthwise, and then in half again. Tape ends together and attached to the side of the pot. Flip the pot over and wear as a hat.

Students will enjoy the curious looks they get walking around school like Johnny Appleseed.

Apple Stamps

Apple halves or slices make great stamps. Place some tempera paint in a shallow pan. Slice an apple in half, and dip the inside part into the paint. Press apple stamps onto a piece of paper. Cut the apples into slices for different stamps. Using various colors, turn this art project into a patterning activity. Hint: When slicing the apples, try to make the cut as level as possible, so the resulting apple slice will be flat for the best prints.

Apple-Seed Pictures

Start collecting apple seeds long before doing this project. Use the seeds to make mosaics. Have students fill in parts of a picture with apple seeds. Or, students can use the seeds in a diagram of how an apple tree grows.

I Can Make a Difference

Johnny Appleseed is said to have made the world a better place by planting trees, although some people thought he was odd. Copy this pattern on red paper for each student. Brainstorm with students ways they can make the world a better place. Have each child complete this sentence on his or her apple shape: *I'm just one person, but I can....* Later, discuss how individuals come together to make the world a better place.

Estimating and Counting Seeds

Materials:
(for each child)

- apple
- plastic knife
- paper plate
- sandwich bag

Ask students to describe what an apple seed looks like. Start them thinking about the size of an apple seed by asking for size comparisons with other objects (e.g., "It's smaller than a raisin, but bigger than a grain of sand."). Ask each student to estimate how many seeds are in their apples. Write responses on paper plates. Have each student count the seeds in his or her apple by cutting it in half and picking out the seeds. Check estimations against the actual amount of seeds in each apple. Identify estimations that were close or reasonable. Keep the seeds in individual sandwich bags for later learning activities.

An Apple for the Student

Take this opportunity to reverse roles by giving apples to your students. Discuss the tradition of students bringing an apple for their teacher as a sign of affection and respect. Explain how your classroom is a place of mutual respect. Give an apple to your students one at a time, and say why you are giving the apple (e.g., "Troy, I'm giving you this apple because your smile lights up the room." "Jenny, I'm giving you this apple because you are a math whiz.").

Storytelling

The line between fact and fiction is fuzzy regarding Johnny Appleseed. Did he really walk around in his bare feet, wearing a cooking pot on his head? After his death, a newspaper started reporting on the life of Johnny Appleseed. Stories were passed from person to person, and many were embellished along the way. Have fun playing this storytelling game with your students. Have students sit in a circle, and invite one child to begin a story by saying one sentence and beginning another. He or she then stops in mid-sentence and allows the next child to pick up where he or she left off. For example:

Student 1 - "Once there was a dog as big as a horse. He was nice enough, except when he…"

Student 2 - "…drooled on your head, which was gross. In fact, one day he drooled on…"

Johnny Appleseed Messages

This variation on the "telephone" game starts with students sitting in a line. The first person whispers something to the next person in line. In this game, students will talk about Johnny Appleseed. The listener then repeats the message to the next person in line, and so on, until the message has made it's way to the end of the line. Make the first message silly, such as "Johnny Appleseed dropped the pot off his head and onto his bare feet." Enjoy the laughter when the last person announces out loud the message which was most likely distorted through the process. Discuss how stories change when passed from person to person.

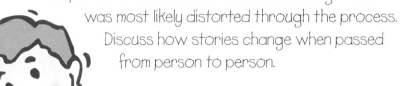

Cooking Pot Relay

Divide the class into two teams. Give each team a cooking pot to be held upside down with ten seeds on top. Have the first student from each team run a designated distance without dropping any seeds. When the players return, two more team members take the pot and run the same distance. If a player drops any seeds, he or she must pick them up, return to the starting line, and begin again.

Squatter's Game

Johnny Appleseed was a squatter. A squatter is someone who comes upon a piece of unoccupied land and claims it for him or herself. In certain parts of the world, "squatters' rights" still exist. Set up chairs as if playing musical chairs, setting out one less chair than students. Play music, and invite students to march around the chairs. When the music stops, have the students squat with their hands on the chairs. The student left without a chair leaves the group, and one chair is removed. Play continues until only one child remains squatting in front of a chair.

Applesauce

Applesauce never tastes as good as when it's made in the classroom. This simple recipe is sure to please your students' noses and tummies.

Ingredients:
apples
honey, lemon juice, cinnamon

Materials:
paper plates
plastic knives
large cooking pot

Either peel or have your students peel apples. Then cut the apples into small pieces and place them in the cooking pot. An apple peeler/corer can also be used to break apples into small pieces. Cook over medium heat, stirring periodically until the apples are soft. Add water only if apples seem dry. Add honey for sweetness, lemon for tartness and cinnamon for taste.

Dried Apples

Wash and remove the cores from apples. Place a 12" (30cm) piece of string through the center of each apple and tie. Hang apples outside to dry in a safe place free from bugs. Remove strings and slice the dried apples. Serve as a tasty, healthy snack.

22

Grandparents' Day

- Flower Centerpieces
- Sachets
- Picture Frames
- A Moment in Time
- Pinch Pots
- "When I Was Young . . ."

- Acrostic Poem
- Songfest
- Games That Span Generations
- Fact vs. Fiction
- Cookies with Grandparents

Grandparents' Day   Decorations

Flower Centerpieces

Grandparents will love these pretty centerpieces which can be dismantled and sent home with your students' grandparents. Have each student make four handprints, with fingers together, using tempera paint on white construction paper. Vary the color from student to student, but keep each individual set of handprints the same color. After the handprints dry, cover the outside of a large coffee can with plain paper for students to decorate. Or, cover the can with wallpaper or contact paper. Fill the can with sand or dirt and set aside. Next, have each child cut out his or her handprints. Have students roll up a 4" x 12" (10cm x 30cm) piece of green construction paper and tape the ends to make a stem. Attach the four handprints to the stem as petals on a flower. In the center of the flower, glue a small picture of the student, either a photo or a self-drawn portrait. Finish off the flower by tying a ribbon around the stem. Plant about five student "flowers" in a can, and place on desks, tables, or counters.

Sachets

Materials:

(for one sachet)

lace circle with small holes

12" (30cm) piece of ribbon

1 teaspoon (5ml) potpourri

Spoon potpourri over center of lace. Gather ends together and tie a ribbon to close the sachet.

Picture Frames

Have the base of the frame ready beforehand, so grandparents can share in finishing these special frames. To make the base, glue four tongue depressors together, leaving a 2 1/2" x 3" (6cm x 7.5cm) space in the center for a picture. At the party, provide students and their grandparents with several small pasta shapes, such as bow-tie pasta or macaroni. Invite students and grandparents to glue pasta pieces around the front side of the frame. Take the frames outside and spray with gold paint. Do not spray frames around students. If necessary, spray-paint the frames after school. Take a Polaroid picture of each student with his or her grandparent(s) to place in the frame for a special souvenir.

Pinch Pots

Pinch pots make great grandparent gifts. To make pinch-pot dough, mix 4 cups (1,000ml) flour, 1 cup (250ml) salt and about 1/2 cup (125ml) water. Knead until smooth. (This recipe yields eight pinch pots.) Give each child a ball of dough the size of an egg, and have him or her "pinch" the dough into a pot shape. Etch the child's name on the underside of the pot for identification, and bake in a 350-degree oven for one hour. When cool, the pots can be painted with tempera. Wrap and give the pots as-is, or fill with sand or dirt and "plant" plastic flowers inside.

A Moment in Time

At your "Instant Memory" table, set 3–4 bottles of liquid tempera, paper plates, a stack of 9" x 12" (22.5cm x 30cm) white paper, a camera (preferably Polaroid™), glitter, glue, stars, and stickers.

Commemorate your Grandparent's Day Party by creating this scrapbook treasure. Take a photograph of each student with his or her grandparent(s). Invite each family member to place his or her handprint on the paper. Label with names, dates, and anything else they would like to share. Mount the photograph on the paper with glue. What a nice memento!

"When I Was Young..."

Grandparents are a rich source of family history and lore, and most grandparents love to talk about the old days. This activity will open your students' eyes to what life was like when their grandparents were young. Invite children to bring their grandparent(s) to class. Allow each child to introduce his or her grandparent(s), then ask the grandparent(s) to share what school was like when he or she was in the same grade as your students. Stories of friends, dress codes, and pranks are sure to come out. Help students see the similarities as well as the differences between school today and school in the old days.

Acrostic Poem

A few days before the party, create an acrostic poem with the class. Write the letters of the word *grandparent* on a large piece of chart paper. Ask students to think of words that describe grandparents that correspond with each letter. For example, "G is for generous," and "R is for reader of books." Make a class acrostic poem and invite students to read it to their grandparent guests. Students can take turns reading the lines of the poem in twos or threes, giving all children a chance to participate.

Songfest

Treat your grandparent guests to a songfest. Begin practicing several weeks beforehand. Songs about love and caring are good to choose, as well as classic songs grandparents might be familiar with. About 10-15 minutes of songs is ideal for a party setting.

Grandparents' Day   Game

Games That Span Generations

Your students' grandparents have fond memories of marbles, jacks, yo-yos, and jump ropes. Put these objects at a station, and let grandparent/grandchild duos enjoy playing together. Encourage grandparents to share other games from their youth with their grandchildren. Pick one game that sounds feasible, and play it with your students.

Fact vs. Fiction

Grandparents have done some amazing things in their lifetimes. Ask each grandparent to think of one amazing thing he or she has done. Ask grandparents to also create one tall tale of something they have done. Each grandparent takes a turn standing up and telling the factual event and the fictional tale, without identifying which is which. Let students guess which story is fact and which is fiction.

Cookies with Grandparents

Cooking together is a great way to spend quality time with grandparents. For this activity, pre-mix or buy ready-made cookie dough. Tape down waxed paper and give each grandparent/child pair some cookie dough in a plastic gallon bag. Let pairs knead the dough and roll it out together. Have cookie cutters (or plastic cups to make circles) available. Cookies can be decorated with sugar or sprinkles. Pop into the oven and enjoy later in the party.

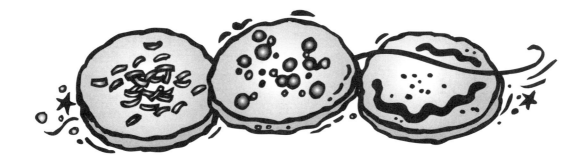

Halloween

- Ghost Pencil Favors
- Pumpkin Words
- Making Masks
- Halloween Pillowcases
- Candy-Corn Dispensers
- Ghost Wind Socks
- Spooky Hands

- Decorate a Pumpkin
- A Witch Story
- Pumpkin Patch
- Pumpkin-Seed Math
- Weighing a Pumpkin
- Monster March
- Halloween Bingo

- Roll the Pumpkin
- Booooo . . . BOOOOO!
- Beanbag Toss
- Pumpkin Obstacle Course
- All Rise
- Pumpkin Cookie Decorating
- Toasted Pumpkin Seeds

Halloween   Decorations

Ghost Pencil Favors

Students will love these "boo"-tiful Halloween party favors. Make a ball with one facial tissue and tape it to the eraser end of an unsharpened Halloween pencil. Drape another tissue over the ball and tie a 6" (15cm) piece of yarn at the bottom of the ball to make a little ghost. Use a black marker to make eyes and a mouth. Kids love to twist the pencil back and forth between their palms and watch their ghosts "fly."

Pumpkin Words

Spell any word you choose by carving the words out of a pumpkin. Most words will wrap around the pumpkin, so students will need to walk around it to read the whole word. Some Halloween expressions such as "aaah" or "eeek" can lead to discussions on short and long vowel sounds.

Making Masks

Masks can be made several ways, such as with large paper grocery bags or paper plates. In any case, make sure eye holes are large enough and positioned appropriately so the student can see out of the mask. Be sure to also make plenty of space at the mouth area for breathing. For paper-bag masks, cover the whole bag with white paper for decorating. Cut the bag so it is shoulder length when worn. Glue a popsicle stick at the bottom of the paper-plate mask for holding. Provide yarn, sequins, glitter, paint, feathers, buttons, and other art supplies for decorating.

Halloween Pillowcases

Start collecting pillowcases long before Halloween. (Most parents are willing to part with an old pillowcase.) Stick with solid colors, preferably white. Communicate to parents that this Halloween pillowcase can be used year after year. Halloween pillowcases can be decorated with fabric paint or permanent marker. Best results are attained when pillowcases are tacked tightly to a large piece of cardboard.

Candy-Corn Dispensers

Cut two pieces of orange felt using the pumpkin pattern. Glue the sides together, leaving a space at the stem. Precut or have students cut eyes, noses, and mouths to glue on to make jack-o'-lanterns. Let glue dry. Fill jack-o'-lanterns with candy corns through the stem. Simply squeeze the jack-o'-lantern to pop out a candy corn! Students can also make candy-corn dispensers to give as Halloween gifts for family and friends.

Ghost Wind Socks

Materials:

2 sheets 9" x 12" (22.5cm x 30cm) white construction paper

6"–20" (15cm x 50cm) strips white crepe paper

1 sheet 6" x 9" (15cm x 22.5cm) black construction paper

1'–3' (30.5cm–1m) string or yarn pieces

glue sticks

scissors

hole punch

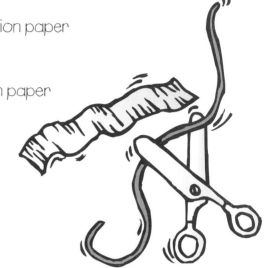

(cont'd)

Ghost Wind Socks - continued

Instructions:

1) Glue both white papers together at the short sides to make a cylinder.

2) Cut out a mouth and two (or more) eyes for the ghost from black construction paper.

3) Glue the eyes and mouth on the cylinder.

4) Glue crepe-paper strips just inside the bottom of the ghost, about 2" (5cm) apart.

5) With a hole punch, punch two holes at the top of the ghost on each side where the papers overlap.

6) Run the string between the holes and tie at the top.

Spooky Hands

Students will enjoy creating and eating this craft project.

Materials:

(for one hand)

- plastic surgical glove
- 5 candy corns
- cooled popped popcorn to fill glove
- spider ring
- 12" (30cm) string or yarn piece

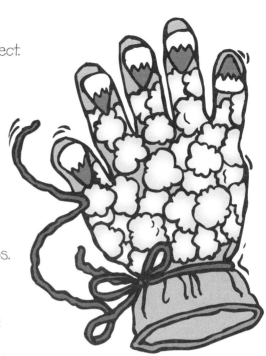

Place the candy corns inside the glove at the fingertips. Fill glove with popcorn and tie closed at the end with string. Slip the spider ring on one finger. Let students take their spooky hands home to display and eat later.

Decorate a Pumpkin

Pumpkins can be great canvases for art. They can be painted with tempera paint and/or objects can be added to them. Some supplies to provide for decorating pumpkins are yarn, buttons, cereal pieces, raisins, leaves, twigs, fabric scraps, licorice vines, and other small objects. Place students in small groups, and invite them to decorate their pumpkins together. Make sure students give their pumpkins a name. Have a contest to determine winners in categories such as "Scariest," "Silliest," "Most Creative," and so on.

A Witch Story

Fold a piece of orange 9" x 12" (22.5cm x 30cm) construction paper in half horizontally ("hamburger" fold), and tell this story orally while cutting out shapes on the paper:

Miss Witch was looking for a new home after a fight with her neighbor, Mr. Jack-o'-Lantern. She really wanted a black home, but there were none to be found. She stumbled across this orange home (hold up folded paper), but it was definitely a "fixer upper." "A house without eaves. How can that be?" Miss Witch cried, as she waved her hands (cut a small triangle out of each top corner on the unfolded edge) and made some eaves. "It's a fine enough house now," said Miss Witch, "but how do I get in?" She mumbled some magic words and made herself a door (cut a rectangle door on the lower right unfolded edge). She went in her house and

(cont'd)

A Witch Story - continued

looked around. She liked the house very much, but it was too dark inside, even for a witch. "I need a window," she said, and with a turn of a spell, a window was added to the witch's home. (Cut a square in the middle of the left side of the house.) She was happy in her house, but a little lonely. "I shall make a cat door for my cat," she cackled. (Cut a triangle out of the bottom of the unfolded half, in the middle). Miss Witch was at last happy in her new home, until she discovered Mr. Jack-O-Lantern had followed her after all (unfold paper to display a jack-o'-lantern).

Older students can cut their own papers as the story is told. Younger students can identify the shapes as they are cut out.

Pumpkin Patch

If you are giving your students pumpkins or mini-pumpkins (squash) for Halloween, consider displaying them in a "pumpkin patch." Make vines by twisting green construction or tissue paper and placing it between the pumpkins. Scatter real or paper leaves throughout the patch. Discuss what to look for when picking a pumpkin, and let your students "pick" a pumpkin to keep at the end of the party. Purchase a few extra pumpkins so that the last student to choose doesn't feel he or she got the "dud" of the patch.

Pumpkin-Seed Math

Work with a large group or small groups to find out how many seeds are in a pumpkin. First, take all estimates and write them on chart paper. Try to write the estimates in descending order, leaving space for other estimates. Cut the top off the pumpkin and let students take turns pulling out the seeds. Ask them to describe the difference between how a pumpkin feels on the outside and the inside. Rinse the seeds in a colander and lay out on paper towels to dry. Students can place the seeds in rows of ten, and put ten rows in bowls to make groups of 100 for easier counting. Go back and check estimations, looking for those that were close or reasonable. Save the seeds for toasting or other math activities.

Weighing a Pumpkin

Pumpkins come in all sizes, which makes them good items for estimating and measuring weight. Before weighing any pumpkins, however, weigh several larger or smaller objects to introduce students to the concept of weight. Use three pumpkins of various sizes. First, take estimates of the medium-sized pumpkin's weight. Write all the estimates on chart paper in descending order, leaving space for other estimates. Weigh the pumpkin and discuss if the estimates were reasonable. Follow the same procedure with the larger and smaller pumpkins, making note of their relative size.

Monster March

If your students wear costumes to school on Halloween, show them off by forming a costume parade. Walk the parade through the school office, around the playground when other students are out, and/or any other place where people might enjoy seeing your students and where student-learning would not be disrupted. If parading on a schoolwide basis, a time can be set aside for older students to come out of their classrooms to watch the younger students walk through the halls. Pipe in a recording of "Monster Mash" through the loudspeaker to add to the fun. The whole parade takes less than 20 minutes.

Reproducible

Halloween Bingo

Play Bingo, using candy corn as counters. Or, make Halloween-themed Bingo cards. Have each student draw lines dividing a paper into fourths. Have students cut out four pictures from magazines, and glue one in each section of the paper. Extra pictures can be saved in an envelope for another day. The first student to fill up a Halloween Bingo card with four candy corns wins.

Roll the Pumpkin

Pumpkins don't roll straight, which makes this game good for belly laughs. Have students take turns rolling a pumpkin to each other. When a student catches the pumpkin, he or she gives clues about what his or her costume will be. When someone guesses the costume, it's time to roll the pumpkin to someone else.

Reproducible　　　37

Booooo . . . BOOOOO!

The object of this game is to find a hidden "ghostie." Make a ghostie by balling up a piece of facial tissue and draping another piece of facial tissue over the ball. Secure with a rubber band or piece of string at the bottom of the ball. Add eyes and a mouth with black marker. The game starts with one student closing his or her eyes while ghostie hides with another student. When the first student opens his or her eyes and begins to look for ghostie, invite the class to give clues telling if he or she is "hot" or "cold." If the student is far from ghostie, the class says "booooo" very quietly. As the student gets closer, the "BOOOO" gets louder until the student guesses who has ghostie.

Beanbag Toss

Using the pattern for candy-corn dispensers, make pumpkin beanbags. Sew the edges instead of gluing them, and fill them with uncooked beans or rice. Draw a large jack-o'-lantern with a wide open mouth on a sturdy piece of cardboard. Make a game out of tossing the beanbags into the jack-o'-lantern's mouth.

Pumpkin Obstacle Course

For this game, you will need one large pillowcase and four pumpkins with the stems cut off. You may wish to paint a pumpkin on the pillowcase beforehand. Make an obstacle course any way you'd like with the four pumpkins. Divide the class into two relay teams, and time each team as they run through the course. To make it through the course, students must step into the pillowcase and hop around the pumpkins, as if he or she was a pumpkin hopping through a patch.

All Rise

Children love this activity which gives them a chance to recall past Halloweens. Have students place their chairs in a circle, with one student standing in the middle without a chair. The student in the middle says, "All rise who have been a _____ for Halloween." The student then fills in the blank with any typical costume such as a ghost, witch, bride, dog, and so on. All students who have worn that costume for Halloween at one time or another stand up and sit in any empty chair. The person in the middle finds an empty chair, too. The last person standing without a chair gets to stand in the middle and name the next costume.

Pumpkin Cookie Decorating

Materials:

1 pumpkin-shaped cookie per child

vanilla frosting

yellow and red food coloring

plastic knives

decorating items (chocolate chips, red hots, sprinkles, raisins, and so on)

Invite students to help color the frosting to see how yellow and red make orange.

Toasted Pumpkin Seeds

Make use of the seeds after carving a pumpkin. Separate the seeds from the pulp and rinse them in a colander. Place seeds in a mixing bowl and add up to two tablespoons (30ml) vegetable oil. Arrange seeds in a single layer on an ungreased cookie sheet, and sprinkle with salt. Cook in a preheated 300-degree oven for 30 minutes, or until slightly brown.

Thanksgiving

- Pinecone Turkeys
- Fall Leaf Centerpiece
- Native American Vests, Headbands, and Necklaces
- We Are Thankful
- Thanksgiving Placemats
- Disguise a Turkey

- Thanks Bulletin Board
- Corn Mosaics
- Orange Pomander Balls
- Hand Turkeys
- Family Feast
- Thankful Presentation
- Beanbag Turkey Toss

- Turkey Calling Contest
- Find the Turkey
- "Turkey" Sandwiches
- Cornbread Muffins
- Native American Fry Bread
- Individual Pumpkin Pies
- Not-Too-Hot Maple Cider

Pinecone Turkeys

Materials:

(for one turkey)

    pinecone

    three 4" (10-cm) pipe cleaners

    two 6" x 12" (15cm x 30cm) wallpaper scraps

    feathers

    glue

Instruct students to glue the backs of both pieces of wallpaper together and set it aside to dry. Have students turn their pinecones sideways and use pipe cleaners to make turkey legs and a head. Use real colored feathers or let students cut out their own feather shapes out of the wallpaper scraps. Invite children to glue feathers onto their pinecones to make colorful turkeys.

Fall Leaf Centerpiece

This project takes several days to complete.

Materials:
(for one centerpiece)
- glass bowl
- newspaper strips
- papier-mâché paste
- paintbrush
- petroleum jelly
- fall-colored (purple, brown, green, orange) tissue-paper squares
- clear nail polish

Coat the underside of the glass bowl with petroleum jelly and place it upside down. Dip strips of newspaper into papier-mâché paste and completely cover bottom and outer sides of the bowl. Brush papier-mâché paste over the newspaper and add another layer of strips. Let dry for four hours. Repeat two more times. Remove hardened newspaper from bowl and add a layer of newspaper over the petroleum jelly. Let dry and trim edges. Paste two layers of tissue-paper squares all over bowl. When dry, coat with clear nail polish. Fill the bowl with fall leaves for a beautiful fall display.

Thanksgiving

Costume

Native American Vests, Headbands, and Necklaces

Vests – You will need a large paper grocery bag for each vest. Cut an opening in the middle, and cut out armholes and a collar. Leave the "fringing" to the kids. Give students scissors and let them cut the fringe on the bottom of the "vests." With cutout shapes and markers, invite students to decorate their vests. Supply pictures of real Native American dress for inspiration.

Headbands – Give each student a strip of adding-machine tape big enough to go around his or her head. Supply paper shapes such as circles, triangles, squares, ovals, rectangles, and diamonds in a variety of colors. Have students glue the shapes in patterns on the tape, and glue the ends together.

Necklaces – Give each student a length of string. Have him or her wrap a piece of tape around each end of the string to help with beading. Buy a variety of beads at a local craft store, and let students create their own necklaces. Again, provide pictures for inspiration, and encourage students to create patterns in their beading.

We Are Thankful

Make a tree or bulletin board of thanks. Give each child a 9" x 12" (22.5cm x 30cm) piece of red, yellow, brown, orange, or purple construction paper. Ask students to fold their papers vertically ("hot dog" fold). On the folded edge, have students write their names with the letters touching the fold. They then draw a squiggly line around the bumps of their names. Have students cut around the squiggly line, but not on the fold. Unfolding the paper makes a fall leaf that is unique to each child. Write one thing the child is thankful for on the blank side of the leaf. Show each leaf to the class, and let students guess to whom the leaf belongs. Display the leaves by hanging them on a tree or a bulletin board.

Thanksgiving Placemats

Personalized placemats can be used at classroom feasts and/or sent home for Thanksgiving dinner with the family. To make placemats, have students cut fall leaves from red, yellow, orange, brown, and purple construction paper. On each fall leaf, students can either write or draw a picture of one thing they are thankful for. Magazine cut-outs can also be used. Students then glue leaves to a 12" x 18" (30cm x 45cm) sheet of construction paper. Laminate the placemats, allowing students to use them year after year.

Disguise a Turkey

Copy this turkey and let your students' imaginations soar with this transformation activity. Tell students that Terry Turkey does not want to be found before Thanksgiving. Have them turn this line drawing of a turkey into something else, in order to hide Terry Turkey. Have a contest, rewarding best disguise.

Thanks Bulletin Board

This bulletin board will remind students of what Thanksgiving is all about. Have each child trace and cut out two handprints in various fall colors—purple, green, brown, yellow, and orange. Arrange the handprints on the bulletin board to spell the word "Thanks."

Corn Mosaics

Uncooked popcorn can be used to make beautiful fall mosaics. Invite students to create line drawings, and fill in one or several parts of the drawings with unpopped kernels. The kernels can be left as is, or painted after the glue dries.

Orange Pomander Balls

In colonial times, pomanders were used to hide unpleasant kitchen smells. Make these orange pomander balls with your students.

Materials:
(for one ball)

orange	cinnamon
whole cloves	cheesecloth
large paper clip	12" (30cm) piece of ribbon

Open up a paper clip, and stick both ends in the top of the orange. Stick cloves close together all around the orange, taking care not to puncture the skin between cloves. Roll the orange in a dish of cinnamon and wrap in the cheesecloth, leaving the paper clip exposed. Tie cheesecloth ends around the paper clip with the ribbon. Students will need to store these at home for two to three weeks in a cool, dry place until the orange hardens. Once hardened, the orange pomander ball can be placed in a drawer or closet to give a fresh fall scent.

Hand Turkeys

The outline of a hand can be used to make turkeys in several different ways, with the fingers as the turkey's feathers and the thumb as the turkey's head. Keep it simple by tracing children hands and letting them decorate by coloring. Or, trace students' hands onto brown construction paper, cut them out, and glue onto another paper to make a picture. You can also make a class mural of a turkey village with the cutout hands.

Thanksgiving

Activity

Family Feast

Why not share your Thanksgiving party with students' families? Send out invitations about a month in advance to give working parents a chance to attend. Most of the food can be prepared by students beforehand, and planning party activities need not be elaborate. The point of a family feast is for students and parents to spend quality time together at school.

Thankful Presentation

Touch your students' parents' hearts with this presentation. Cut out the letters to the words *I am thankful!* out of 12" x 18" (30cm x 45cm) brown construction paper. Two students can hold up each letter for 24 students. If you have more students, triple the students up on some letters or add more exclamation points. Before the family feast, have students think about what they are thankful for concerning their parents. Students can jot their thoughts on the back of the letters they are holding. At the feast, have students stand in a line, keeping the letters and words in order. The student(s) holding the letter *I* raises his or her letter and tells what he or she is thankful for. Continue until all students have spoken and all letters are raised.

Beanbag Turkey Toss

Draw a large turkey on a sturdy piece of cardboard, color it, and cut it out. Cut a hole in the middle of the turkey's belly. Use premade beanbags, or make some in the shape of a turkey, using a turkey cookie cutter as a pattern. Make a game out of tossing the beanbags into the turkey's belly.

Find the Turkey

The object of this game is to find Terry Turkey. Terry Turkey can be a picture or small toy turkey. The game starts with one student closing his or her eyes while Terry Turkey is hidden with another student. When the first student opens his or her eyes and begins to look for Terry Turkey, the class give clues, telling if he or she is "hot" or "cold." If the student is far from Terry Turkey, the class says "gobble, gobble" very quietly. As the student gets closer, the "GOBBLE, GOBBLE" gets louder until the student guesses who has Terry Turkey.

Turkey Calling Contest

Such a contest has actually been going on for over half a century in one part of the country. Hold your own "First Annual Turkey Calling Contest." Have students, squat, walk, and flap their arms, all while making turkey noises. Vote on the best caller, or turn the activity into a running relay race with two or more teams.

"Turkey" Sandwiches

Using turkey-shaped cookie cutters, have students cut out turkey-shaped pieces of bread and slip a slice of turkey sandwich meat in between the pieces. Have available both whole wheat and white bread, and let your guests add mayonnaise and mustard as they wish. Can't find turkey cutters? Invite students to make simple finger sandwiches by cutting circles, triangles, squares, and rectangles from the bread with plastic knives.

Cornbread Muffins

Children fall into two groups concerning cornbread—those who love it and those who haven't tried it yet. Cornbread can be made easily with cornbread mix from the grocery store. Instead of cornbread, make corn muffins by pouring the batter into paper baking cups in muffin tins. Bake according to package directions.

Native American Fry Bread

Ingredients:

- 3 cups (750ml) flour
- 1 teaspoon (5ml) vinegar
- 1 teaspoon (5ml) salt
- 1 cup (250ml) milk
- 4 teaspoons (20ml) baking powder
- cinnamon sugar
- vegetable oil

Materials:

- mixing bowl
- small bowl
- mixing spoon
- measuring cups
- measuring spoons
- electric skillet
- plastic knife
- spatula

(cont'd)

Native American Fry Bread – continued

Mix flour, salt and baking powder by hand in mixing bowl. Combine vinegar and milk in smaller bowl. Add the smaller bowl's ingredients to the dry ingredients. Mix together to form a dough. Roll dough onto a floured surface. Cut into strips. Fry in vegetable oil in electric skillet. Sprinkle with cinnamon sugar. Serves eight. Helpful Hint: The thinner the dough is rolled out, the lighter and flakier the bread.

Individual Pumpkin Pies

Ingredients:
(for eight pies)

    8 mini pie shells (ready-made)
    canned pumpkin pie filling, prepared as directed on can

Instead of cooking one big pie, pour the pumpkin mix into mini pie shells, which are sold at most grocery stores. Bake according to directions on can.

Not-Too-Hot Maple Cider

This beverage will not only taste yummy, but will fill your classroom with the aroma of fall. Combine 4 cups (1,000ml) apple cider, two tablespoons (30ml) maple syrup, and one cinnamon stick in a crock pot. Let sit on low for at least 20 minutes before serving. Parents attending the family feast may be the best customers for this autumn drink. Take the cider outside if weather permits so students can enjoy the warm cider in the cool, crisp air.

Winter

- Cultural Displays
- Snow Storm
- Family Ornaments
- Holiday Countdown Chains
- Holiday Soaps
- Santa Wind Socks

- Personalized Wrapping Paper
- Winter Houses
- Snow
- Letters to Santa
- Family Traditions
- Secret Pal Exchange

- The Dreidel Game
- Snowflake Descriptions
- Freeze and Melt
- Snowflake Matchup
- Senegalese Cookies
- Potato Latkes

Winter	Decorations

Cultural Displays

Make your winter party inclusive by displaying decorations from a variety of cultural traditions. For Christmas, display a small Christmas tree or paper trees decorated with colorful circles. Include Hanukkah by putting out a menorah, or by making one out of paper. Represent Kwanzaa by obtaining or making a bendera, which is a flag with a green stripe on the bottom, a black stripe in the middle, and a red stripe on the top.

Reproducible

Snow Storm

Turn your classroom into a winter wonderland by hanging snowflakes around the room. Make a snowflake by folding a white paper circle in half, and then in half again. Make little cuts with scissors out of the sides of the folded circle. Unfold the circle to see a pretty snowflake. Hang the snowflakes with fishing line of different lengths for the appearance of falling snow.

Family Ornaments

Copy and send home this letter to parents:

Dear Parents,

Holiday time is a special time for families. We would like to have your family represented on our class tree. Your family homework assignment is to create an ornament together for your child to bring to school. Keep the ornament small, under 5" (12.5cm) in length and width, and make sure your family name is somewhere on the ornament. Keep it simple, but try to have all family members participate in its design. Thank you in advance for your contribution.

Yours truly,

Hang the family ornaments on a small, leafless tree or a bulletin board. Send them home before winter break.

Holiday Countdown Chains

Help your students deal with holiday anticipation while sharpening calendar skills. Students can make a countdown chain for Christmas, Hanukkah, Kwanzaa, or any other holiday by connecting strips of 1" x 4" (2.5cm x 10cm) colored paper in a chain. The colors can correspond to the particular holiday, such as red and green for Christmas. Encourage creative patterning with the colors. On a calendar, put a sticker on the holiday. Cover today's date with your hand, and count how many days until the holiday. Make a chain with that many links. Students can take one link off the chain on the next day and continue to do so until the holiday arrives. One link will remain the day before the holiday, signaling one more day left to wait!

Holiday Soaps

Your students can make holiday soaps to give as gifts to mom and dad. You will need Christmas, Hanukkah, and generic-flowered wrapping paper for this project. You will also need one bar of plain white soap for each child and some melted wax. Have students cut a picture from wrapping paper and glue it on the smooth side of the soap. The smooth side of the soap is then dipped into hot melted wax by an adult, and placed on waxed paper to dry. When cool, the decorative soap is ready to be given as a gift.

Santa Wind Socks

Materials:

(for one wind sock)

2 sheets of 9" x 12" (22.5cm x 30cm) tan, peach, beige or brown construction paper for Santa's face

6" x 9" (15cm x 22.5cm) sheet of white construction paper

3-foot (1m) string or yarn piece

six 20" (50cm) white crepe paper strips

glue stick

scissors

hole punch

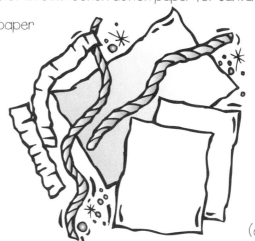

(cont'd)

Santa Wind Socks - continued

Instructions:

1) Glue the paper for Santa's face together at the short sides to make a wide cylinder.

2) Cut Santa's hat from red paper, eyes from black paper (see pattern) and mustache and ball for hat from white paper.

3) Glue all the pieces on the cylinder, making sure Santa's mustache reaches the bottom of the paper.

4) Glue crepe paper strips just inside the bottom of the cylinder, about 2" (5cm) apart.

5) Punch a hole at the top of the cylinder on each side where the edges overlap.

6) Run the string between the two holes and tie at the top.

Reproducible

55

© Fearon Teacher Aids FE7956

Personalized Wrapping Paper

Invite students to create wrapping paper to wrap holiday gifts. Provide each child with a three foot (1m) piece of butcher paper. Cut stamps out of sponges in the shapes of stars, Christmas trees, dreidels, and other holiday shapes. Put various colors of tempera paint in shallow pans, and have students decorate their papers with the stamps. Let the paper dry, roll it up, and send it home with your students for wrapping gifts at home.

Winter Houses

This fun craft project is made easier with some preplanning. Two weeks before your winter party, ask parents for donations of ten boxes of powdered sugar, paper plates, 1 box of graham crackers for every four children, licorice vines, red hot candies, sticks of colorful gum, pretzel sticks, spice drops, chocolate chips, marshmallows, large and small candy canes, cookie sprinkles, shredded coconut, and waxed paper. Collect enough 8-oz. (250ml) milk cartons for each student to use one as a base. Rinse the milk cartons out well and let them dry. At least a day before the party, students can make the base to their winter house by taping closed the milk carton, covering it with waxed paper, and attaching graham cracker pieces around the sides and on the top with powdered sugar "glue." Make powdered sugar glue by mixing powdered-sugar with water until it becomes a pasty consistency. At the party, use the rest of the ingredients, along with more powdered-sugar glue, to decorate the winter houses.

Snow

Have a cool winter party with snow. Instead of hoping for a blizzard, order snow from a local ice company. You can order an amount ranging from a small mound to a big hill to give your students a firsthand experience with snow. Ordering snow for your school's playground can be less costly than a field trip, and a big hill can be shared by several classes—two points to bring up when looking for funding from your principal or parent group.

Letters to Santa

If your winter celebration includes Santa, have students address letters to Santa several weeks before your party. Recruit older students at your school to write back to your students as Santa. Provide beautiful stationery for Santa's "replies." Remind older students to write in manuscript and keep their replies simple. Santa's letters can arrive at your winter party, where you can watch your students' eyes grow wide with wonder.

Family Traditions

To give your students a better view of the various ways families celebrate holidays, invite a few parents to come in to explain their holiday traditions. It's difficult to teach about a holiday if you don't celebrate yourself, so leave it to the experts. Encourage parents to bring in food or treats associated with the holiday they are presenting. In addition, assign homework for your students to write with their families about one family tradition in their homes. Another option is to take students on a walking tour to several students' houses that are close to school and decorated for different winter holidays.

Secret Pal Exchange

Gift giving is an integral part of most winter holiday celebrations. Your students can exchange handmade gifts with a "secret pal." A week or two before your winter party, have students draw names for a secret pal gift exchange. Keep track of who picks who, and have on hand some spare gifts for students whose pals don't make gifts. On the days following the name-drawing, remind students periodically to work on their pal's gift. You can decide whether or not to reveal secret pal names after the gift exchange.

The Dreidel Game

Celebrate Hanukkah by playing with dreidels. Make a dreidel by covering a milk carton with construction paper. Write one of these words on each side: *Nun* (nothing), *Gimmel* (all), *Hey* (half), and *Shin* (put in). Press an unsharpened pencil through the top and out the bottom of the carton. Play The Dreidel Game in groups of four to six, with each person starting with a dozen of any small objects, such as pennies or cereal pieces. The game starts with each person putting one object into the "pot" between all the players. Each player takes a turn spinning the dreidel. If the word *Nun* appears, the player does nothing. If the word *Gimmel* shows, the player takes everything in the pot. When this happens, all the other players pitch in an object to get the pot started again. If the word *Hey* appears, the player takes half of the pot, or half plus one if there are an odd number of objects in the pot. If the word *shin* is spun, the player adds two objects to the pot. Play continues until one player has all the objects.

Snowflake Descriptions

Take ten of the snowflake pairs made for the *Snowflake Matchup* game, and assign each pair a letter. Write the letter on both snowflakes, and split the pairs into two piles, so each pile has a snowflake labeled from A to J. Put two students back to back, and set a pile in front of each. The game is played by having one student guess which snowflake the other student is holding, by listening to a description of it. The first student might say, "This snowflake has a triangle cut off both sides and four heart shapes in the middle." The second student might then say, "Is it snowflake D?" If the correct snowflake is guessed, the first student describes another snowflake. Give each pair a certain amount of time to play, such as two minutes. The winners are the pair that matches the most snowflakes in the allotted time.

Freeze and Melt

Play music and let students dance around the room. When the music stops, students need to freeze right where they are. One student then goes around trying to make at least one other student laugh. When a student laughs, the whole class can "melt" by pretending to be ice cubes melting. The student who laughed is "it" and has to make someone else laugh when the music stops again.

Snowflake Matchup

It's true that no two snowflakes in nature are alike, but they are in this fun game. Make snowflakes as described in Snow Storm Decorations, only fold two circles together to make two identical snowflakes. Use the same-sized circle and create at least ten other pairs of identical snowflakes. In small groups, students can put snowflakes in a paper bag and shake it up. After shaking up the bag, have students empty out the snowflakes onto the ground, making a "snow storm." The student who matches the most pairs is the winner.

60

Reproducible

Senegalese Cookies

Kwanzaa celebrations sometimes include Senegalese cookies. To make Senegalese cookies, spread peanut butter on top of premade sugar cookies. Sprinkle the tops with chopped peanuts. Remember to check if any of your students has a peanut allergy before making these cookies.

Potato Latkes

Introduce your students to the Hanukkah tradition of preparing potato latkes.

Ingredients:

12 potatoes

6 tablespoons (90ml) flour

4 eggs

2 large onions

vegetable oil

2 teaspoons (10ml) salt

1/2 teaspoon (2.5ml) pepper

applesauce

Materials:

mixing bowl

mixing spoon

spatula

grater

blender

paper towels

electric skillet

Wash and grate potatoes. Slice the onion and separate into rings. Blend onion, eggs, salt, pepper, and flour in blender until onions are chopped. Spoon off liquid from the top of the potatoes and combine with the onion mixture. Coat just the bottom of the skillet with vegetable oil and drop in potato mixture by spoonfuls. Loosen the spoonful with a spatula to keep it from sticking. Brown latkes on each side. Let drain on paper towels and serve with applesauce.

Martin Luther King, Jr. Day

- I Have a Dream
- Buddy Peace Posters
- Colorful Crayon Balls
- It Takes All Colors to Make a Rainbow

- Children Have Rights Too
- Guest Speaker
- Problem-Solving Role Plays

- My Hero/Heroine Is . . .
- Follow the Leader
- Peace Squeeze
- Untangle Hands

Martin Luther King, Jr. Day   Decorations

I Have a Dream . . .

Martin Luther King, Jr.'s "I Have a Dream" speech can be a springboard for writing activities in the classroom. Give each student a 8" x 12" (21cm x 30cm) cloud cutout on which to write their dreams for the world. Arrange the clouds on a bulletin board entitled *We Have Dreams*.

Buddy Peace Posters

Students have to cooperate to make buddy peace posters. Write the word *peace* on a 12" x 18" (30cm x 45cm) piece of construction paper for every two students. Instruct student pairs to illustrate a peace poster any way they'd like, with one catch—they both have to have their hands on the same pencil or crayon, and they cannot talk. For an added challenge, pair students with others they don't normally associate with at school.

Colorful Crayon Balls

Make colorful crayon balls to show how bringing different colors together can produce a beautiful result. Collect old crayons and have students peel the paper off. The crayons can be broken into smaller pieces by hand and placed into individual zipper baggies. Put the baggies labeled with students' names on a cookie sheet and place in direct sunlight—long enough to melt the crayons. Or, put the cookie sheet in an oven set on a low heat and watch continuously. Remove when crayons are melted. Make sure the baggies are cool enough for students to touch, but warm enough so the crayons are pliable. Students can mold the crayons into a ball shape while still in the baggies and drop them in a bowl of ice water to harden. After about a minute, remove the crayon balls from the bowl. Peel off the baggies for a fun multicolor crayon.

It Takes All Colors to Make a Rainbow

Create a pattern for a very simple human figure on 8 1/2" x 11" (21cm x 27.5cm) paper. Make ten copies of the pattern on heavy paper, index, or laminated copy paper. Cut them out and set them on a table with pencils, lots of colored paper (wallpaper sample books, too, if you have them), scissors, and tape. During your Martin Luther King, Jr. Day celebration, create a beautiful bulletin board by asking students to stop by the "rainbow table" to trace and cut out some figures for a class project. At the end of the party, arrange the figures into a rainbow shape on the bulletin board entitled "We Are a Rainbow!"

Children Have Rights Too

Martin Luther King, Jr. worked for people's civil rights. Discuss what human rights are with students. Explain that children have rights just like adults. Brainstorm a list of rights that pertain especially to children, such as the right to an education or the right to be treated with respect. Talk specifically about rights your students have in the classroom—the right to be safe and the right to ask questions, for example. Write these rights on a poster and hang it in your classroom.

Guest Speaker

Help Martin Luther King, Jr. Day come alive for your students by bringing a guest speaker into your classroom. Preferably, the speaker would have good knowledge of Dr. King's works, along with the ability to scale down the information to your students' level. Perhaps this person would have experienced some form of discrimination in his or her lifetime. Discuss with the speaker the main points you'd like addressed, such as all humans deserve equality, and conflicts can be resolved peaceably. A simple 15-minute talk with questions will give your students a basic understanding of the struggle for civil rights.

Problem-Solving Role Plays

Role-playing problem-solving increases your students' abilities with this important skill. Call a few students to the front of the class to role-play the following situations:

You hear a friend is saying bad things about you.

Your friend borrows your pencil and breaks it in two.

Someone you know is teasing you.

Someone trips you, and you're not sure if it was an accident.

Someone cuts in front of you in line.

A friend takes something from your lunch without asking.

Someone pushes you.

A friend is gloating about winning.

My Hero/Heroine Is . . .

Martin Luther King, Jr. had heroes who influenced his life, such as Mahatma Gandhi. Brainstorm with your students qualities that make someone a hero or heroine. Make another list of heroes and heroines whom your students admire. Stress that heroes/heroines need not be famous, and may just be the person next door. Also, children can and should be included in the list. Accept all nominations to the list as long as students can justify their answers with qualities from the first list. Invite students to dictate or write about their heroes/heroines, and draw pictures to go along with their writing.

Heroes Heroines

Follow the Leader

Martin Luther King, Jr. was a leader. In honor of him, play a game of "follow the leader." Have each student take a turn leading the class around the classroom, through the school halls, and around the playground. Set a time limit for each leader to lead. Afterward, ask students what it felt like to be a leader. Ask students what made someone a good leader. (e.g., waiting for everyone to catch up, using a sense of humor).

Peace Squeeze

People join hands as a sign of peace and friendship. To play the "peace squeeze" game, students sit in a circle and clasp hands. One person starts the game by squeezing the hand of the person to the right. That person squeezes the next person's hand, and so on, until the squeeze comes back to the person who started it. With a timer or a watch with a second hand, time how long it takes for the squeeze to go around the circle. Set time goals as a group and try to meet them. Send the squeeze in the other direction and see what happens.

Untangle Hands

Create a little conflict in your classroom by playing a game of "untangle hands." Have students stand in circles of six to eight students. Each student reaches across and holds hands with two different students. The challenge is to untangle the group knot without talking. Accomplishing this task requires conflict resolution skills such as patience, cooperation, sense of humor, problem-solving, perseverance, initiative, effort, and caring.

Groundhog Day

- Profile Silhouettes
- Shadow City Skylines
- Groundhog Dramatic Play
- Shadow Walk
- Groundhog Day Predictions
- Tracing Shadow Shapes
- Shadow Tag

Groundhog Day   Arts/Crafts

Profile Silhouettes

Silhouettes can be made by placing a student between a light source, such as a desk lamp or overhead projector, and a wall. Put a black piece of paper on the wall, and have the student stand or sit with his or her profile close to the paper. Draw a line with white chalk around the profile's silhouette. Cut out the silhouette, and mount it on white paper. Don't forget to write the date on this precious keepsake.

Shadow City Skylines

Make a shadow city skyline by water-coloring a 9" x 12" (22.5cm x 30cm) white construction paper with colors of a sunrise (purples and blues) or sunset (oranges and reds). Provide patterns of circles, squares, rectangles, and triangles for students to trace on black paper to make buildings for the skyline. The buildings are then cut out and glued onto the water-colored paper.

Groundhog Dramatic Play

Put five to six student chairs in a circle facing inside. Cover the circle with brown butcher paper to make a groundhog's hole. Divide students into groups of five to act out the groundhog's adventure. One student can act as the groundhog, another as the news reporter covering the action, a third as a photographer, and two more students can serve as onlookers. Each group decides whether the groundhog will or will not see his shadow beforehand and dramatizes the groundhog peeking out of his hole.

Shadow Walk

Groundhog Day is an excellent opportunity to teach about the science of shadows. Kids are naturally curious and amused by shadows. Capitalize on this interest by going on a shadow walk. Of course, the further away from noon time, the longer the shadows. Ask students what they notice about their shadows. Take them out for shadow walks at various times in the same day, and ask them to report their observations.

Groundhog Day Predictions

Predict with your students if the official Punxsutawney Phil will see his shadow and return to his hole for six more weeks of winter weather, or if he will come out and signal an early spring. Poll students and make a graph of their predictions. Choose students to debate both opinions—many will base their opinions on current weather or what they wish would happen. Poll students again to see if any have changed their opinions. Check the midday or evening news to see what the groundhog actually did.

Tracing Shadow Shapes

Give each child a three-foot (1m) piece of butcher paper on which to trace shapes of shadows in nature. Take children outside and let them find shadows of plants to trace. Or, take common classroom objects such as building blocks or items from the housekeeping area to place outside and trace shadows from. When it's close to noon, students can trace each other's shadows in reduced form.

Groundhog Day

Game

Shadow Tag

Play this variation on the game of tag, in which the tagger steps on someone's shadow instead of touching that person to make him or her "it." That person then runs around until stepping on someone else's shadow, making that person the new tagger. Of course, this game is more fun earlier in the morning or later in the afternoon, when shadows are longer and provide more of a target. Lay out boundaries for the game ahead of time, and instruct the tagger to shout "gotcha" when stepping on someone's shadow, as the shadow may be behind him or her.

Valentine's Day

- Heart People
- Valentine Placemats
- "Find a Friend" Necklaces
- Heart Bookmarks
- Baker's Clay Hearts
- Airplane Messages
- Love Stamps

- Valentine Mailboxes
- "Heart Attack"
- Candy Hearts Math
- Love Is . . .
- Classroom Post Office
- Secret Friends
- Which Heart Is Missing?

- Fishing for Hearts
- Who's on My Back?
- Loves Me, Loves Me Not
- Torn Paper Valentines
- Friendship Cookies
- Valentine Sundaes

Valentine's Day

Decorations

Heart People

Cut out large hearts and draw animated faces on the front. Add legs and arms by accordion-pleating strips of white paper. Attach black squares at the ends to make shoes and gloves. Add details such as bow ties and ribbons, and give each heart person a name. Hang heart people with fishing line to give the appearance that they are floating through the classroom.

Valentine Placemats

Teach students how to make valentines by folding a piece of paper in half, drawing half a heart away from the fold, and holding the fold while cutting around the half heart. Once students have mastered this, provide pink, red, white, and purple paper for students to make enough valentines of various sizes to cover a black 12" x 18" (30cm x 45cm) piece of construction paper. These works of art can double as placemats for the Valentine's Day party.

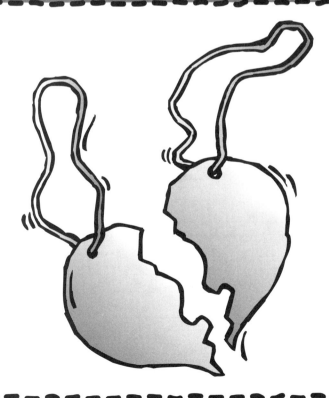

"Find a Friend" Necklaces

Pair off students with new friends by wearing broken heart necklaces. Make two necklaces for each pair by cutting a heart shape from red or pink construction paper, cutting the heart shape in two pieces, and putting each piece on a string to make two separate necklaces. Make sure each heart is cut with a distinct jagged line. Write students' names on the heart pieces. At the party, pass out the necklaces and ask students to find their new friends by putting the heart pieces together.

Heart Bookmarks

Heart bookmarks can be great gifts for Mom or Dad on Valentine's Day. Students can simply cut out small hearts of different colors and glue them on tongue depressors. They can write typical candy heart messages on the hearts and/or tongue depressors, such as *Be mine*, and *Luv ya*.

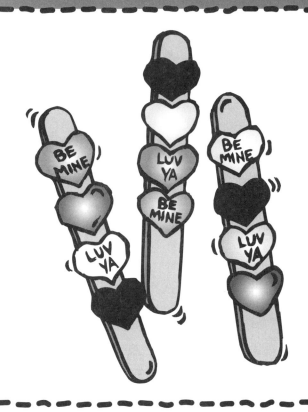

Baker's Clay Hearts

To make baker's clay, mix 4 cups (1,000ml) flour, 1 cup (250ml) salt, and 1/2 cup (125ml) water. Knead until smooth. (This recipe yields eight clay hearts.) Give each child a ball of dough the size of an egg, and let him or her roll it out 1/2" (1cm) thick. Either by molding with hands or using a cookie cutter, have students from the dough into a heart shape. Using a sharp pencil, poke a hole at the top of the and etch the child's name on the bottom side. Bake in a 350-degree oven for one hour. When the hearts cool, they can be painted with tempera paint and a string can be put through the hole for a beautiful valentine ornament.

Airplane Messages

Messages of love are sometimes "painted" across the sky by airplanes. Students can make such messages for their moms and dads on 12" x 18" (30cm x 45cm) blue paper. After writing *I love you* across the paper horizontally, have students glue pieces of cotton over the letters, and a draw an airplane at the end of the words for a clever message of love.

Love Stamps

Invite students to design their own stamps for "mailing" valentines in class. Provide students with 2" x 1" (5cm x 2.5cm) pieces of white paper for stamp making. Obtain a collection of stamps to inspire your students, especially those dealing with love. Talk about stamp collecting as a hobby. Photocopy all the student-made stamps on one or two pieces of paper. Make a copy for each student for his or her letters "sent" in class.

Valentine Mailboxes

Start collecting shoe boxes with lids a couple weeks before Valentine's Day. Cover the boxes with white, pink, or red paper, and cut a slot in the top long enough to fit in valentines and wide enough to accommodate candy that students often exchange. Let students decorate their own mailboxes with stickers, cutout paper and lace hearts, sequins, feathers, and markers or crayons. On the short side of each mailbox, place an index card with the student's name and post office box number displayed. The mailboxes can be placed in order, side by side, for easy mail delivery.

"Heart Attack"

Give your principal, the school secretary, the nurse, or anyone else with a sense of humor, a "heart attack" of the best kind. Find out when the person will be out of his or her office and have your students fill the office with hearts of different sizes, shapes, and colors. Make one big card as a class, explaining that the reason for the "attack" of hearts is because that person is indeed loved.

Candy Hearts Math

Candy hearts make great math manipulatives. Students can estimate, count, pattern, sort and graph with candy hearts, and gobble them up when finished. They can also be used as bingo markers or mosaic pieces. Place candy hearts in a large jar (ten times the number of students you have—24 students = 240 candy hearts), and ask students to estimate how many candy hearts are in the jar. Put a paper baking cup on each child's desk, and place the candy hearts in the cups one at a time until all are counted. Students then have a cup of candy manipulatives for the following activity:

Sweet Math:

I think there are _____ candy hearts in the jar. (estimate)

There were really _____ candy hearts in the jar. (estimate)

_____

I have _____ candy hearts in my cup.

_____ are pink.   _____ are purple.

_____ are yellow.   _____ are white.   (cont'd)

Candy Hearts Math - continued

_____ are green.   _____ are blue.

_____ are orange.   _____ are another color.

pink hearts + purple hearts = _____   yellow hearts + white hearts = _____

green hearts + blue hearts = _____   orange hearts + white hearts = _____

Find a partner and make a pattern with your candy hearts.

Love is . . .

Brainstorm with children ideas of what love is. Give each child a 12" (30cm) heart with the words *Love is* written on one half. The child then writes or dictates on the other side what he or she thinks love really is. Hang children's hearts on a bulletin board entitled *Our Loving Thoughts*.

Valentine's Day   Activity

Classroom Post Office

Turn an area of the classroom into a post office for mailing valentines. Set up the office at least a week before the Valentine's Day party. A refrigerator box or large puppet theater can be used as the post office counter. Place a mailbox for each student behind the "counter," and have students bring in their valentines to put in the mailboxes any time during the week before your party. Consider assigning each child a post office box number and asking your students to correctly address the envelopes. Don't forget to send home a list of your students' names along with their P.O. box number.

Secret Friends

Add a bit of mystery to your Valentine's Day celebration by assigning secret friends. Have students draw names out of a hat. Keep track of the names drawn. Students can periodically put secret messages on top of their secret friends' mailboxes, while trying not to get caught. The notes need not be elaborate. Provide a supply of precut valentine shapes for students to use for secret notes. Send a set of "secret friend" notes yourself so students don't feel left out if their secret friend does not send any notes.

Which Heart Is Missing?

Cut out 31 hearts and write on each a number from 1 to 31. Mix up all the hearts on a table with the numbers facing up, and have students close their eyes. Take one heart away, and have students try to guess which number is missing. For younger students, use only the numbers 1 to 10. For a greater challenge, increase the numbers to 50.

Fishing for Hearts

Take the hearts numbered 1 to 10 from the "Which Heart is Missing?" game and poke a paper clip through the top of each. Make a magnetic fishing pole by tying a magnet to the end of a string and fastening the string to a pole. Place the hearts in a paper grocery bag and play the game in groups of two to four. Each student puts the fishing pole into the bag and slowly brings out a heart. If the heart drops back in the bag, the player loses his or her turn. If a student picks up a heart with the number three, that student earns three points. Play continues until all hearts are out of the bag. The winner is the student with the most points at the end of play.

Who's on My Back?

Write each student's name on a 12" (30cm) heart. Mix up the hearts, and tape them at random on students' backs without letting them see whose name they have. Students then show their backs to other students and ask questions about the person on their back, such as, "Is this person a girl?" or "Is this person wearing white sneakers?" As soon as the student guesses correctly, move the heart to the front of the person whose name was on the heart, making it easier for those who are having difficulty guessing.

80

Reproducible

Loves Me, Loves Me Not

Take the numbers 1 to 10 from the "Which Heart Is Missing?" game and place them in a hat. Have students sit in a circle, while one student draws a number. The number drawn is the number of times the heart will go around the circle. Each time the heart gets passed, the student holding the heart says either "loves me" or "loves me not." The first person to hold the heart always says "loves me," and the second person says "love me not." If the heart ends with "loves me not," that person sits out of the circle. If the heart stops with "loves me," then that person puts the heart back in the bag and picks the next heart to be played. Here's how the game would proceed if the number four was drawn:

Person 1 - "loves me"
Person 2 - "loves me not"
Person 3 - "loves me"
Person 4 - "loves me not"

Person four sits outside the circle. If the game had ended with person three, that person would have stayed in the circle and drawn the next heart. The game, which teaches about odd and even numbers, continues until only one person remains in the circle.

Torn Paper Valentines

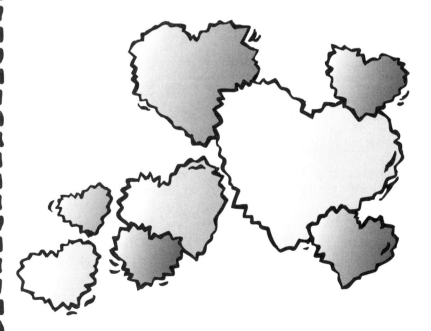

Give each child a 9" x 12" (22.5cm x 30cm) red or pink piece of paper. Ask him or her to tear a heart shape without drawing an outline or using scissors. For an added challenge, have students tear the valentines behind their backs. Make a contest out of this game, or celebrate every attempt for its originality.

Friendship Cookies

Valentine's Day is about friendship, and students can exchange cookies as a way of showing their friendship. Pair off students, perhaps with new friends, and give each pair two premade, plain, heart-shaped cookies. Provide supplies for decorating the cookies, such as pink icing, red hot candies, sprinkles, candy buttons, chocolate kisses and red decorating gel. Have students interview their partners to see what they would like on the cookie. Students can then decorate and enjoy cookies with new friends.

Valentine Sundaes

Provide these *yummy* supplies for a sweet valentine treat:

    strawberry and vanilla ice cream

    strawberry and chocolate topping

    cherries

    chocolate kisses

    chocolate and red sprinkles

    strawberries

    whipped cream

100th Day of School

- Collections of 100
- 100 Stamps
- Where Will 100 Cubes Land?
- Balloon Counting, Sorting, and Graphing
- Flip a Coin

- 100 Physical Activities
- 100 Steps
- Name Patterns
- Balancing Water and Sand
- Rolling Dice to 100
- 100-Second Challenges

100th Day of School   Decorations

Collections of 100

One or two weeks before the 100th day of school, assign "collecting" homework to your students. Ask them to collect and display 100 of any small object—cereal pieces, pennies, popsicle sticks—let their imaginations soar. Ask students to be creative with how they display their objects as well. A word of warning—parents love to take over this project. Communicate to parents the importance of students completing this project on their own, and that student-made projects are the best. Display these collections at your 100th Day of School party.

100 Stamps

Students can practice counting to 100 by putting 100 ink stamps on a 12" x 18" (30cm x 45cm) piece of paper. Offer a variety of stamps and stamp-pad colors. Encourage students to group their stamps by twos, fives, or tens for easier counting. They can jazz up the pictures by making patterns of color, size, or shape of stamp. Remind students to periodically check and recheck the number of stamps they are putting on the paper. These stamp pictures can be swapped for more counting practice or hung on a bulletin board.

Where Will 100 Cubes Land?

If you have 100 Unifix cubes, ask students how long 100 cubes will stretch. Let students place markers with their names on them where they estimate the trail of cubes will end. Measure out the cubes as a class and see whose estimate is the closest. Break the line of cubes into lines of ten, and talk about how ten tens make 100, or how one line of ten is one-tenth of the whole.

Balloon Counting, Sorting, and Graphing

Balloons make colorful, fun manipulatives. Fill your classroom with 100 balloons of various colors. Helium tanks can be rented, or they can be purchased at discount warehouse stores. Three or four adults working together can inflate 100 helium balloons in just under an hour. After your students get over the initial shock of seeing the balloons, the balloons can be counted, sorted, and graphed. They can also be used in math problems, such as *ten purple balloons and four blue balloons equals 14 balloons*. At the end of the day, divide up the balloons and send them home with students. But first, make a balloon bouquet for the school secretary.

Flip a Coin

Introduce probability to students through a simple game of heads or tails. Ask students if a coin were flipped 100 times, how many times would heads come up? How many times would tails show? Take estimates, reminding students that both numbers must add up to 100. For younger students, take just their guess for heads and provide the resulting number for tails. Flip the coin 100 times, keeping tally marks on the overhead projector or chalkboard. Count the tallies. In all probability, the numbers will be pretty close, and if you flipped the coin just a few more times, the result would change again.

100 Physical Activities

Get physical on the 100th day of school. Give your students the chance to do the following activities 100 times:

jump rope

run 100 feet or yards (meters)

toss a beanbag

toss a Frisbee

hop

swing

bounce a ball

hula hoop

touch toes

100th Day of School

Activity

100 Steps

Have students estimate how far 100 steps will take them away from the classroom, each child choosing a different direction for the estimate. Have him or her place a piece of masking tape with his or her name on it on that spot. Let each child trace and cut out his or her foot, and write "100 steps got me here" on the cutout. Place a piece of rolled-up masking tape on the bottom of each cutout. Invite students to take 100 steps in the direction of their estimations, and tape their feet cutouts where 100 steps leads them. Students can then visually compare their estimates with the actual distance.

Name Patterns

Give students blank 100-square charts, and ask them to write their name in the squares, one letter in each square, starting with the upper left-hand corner box. Have them keep writing their names in the remaining squares until all the squares are filled. Ask students to notice the patterns they created by writing their names this way. Let students compare their patterns to those of others, and see if they find any similarities.

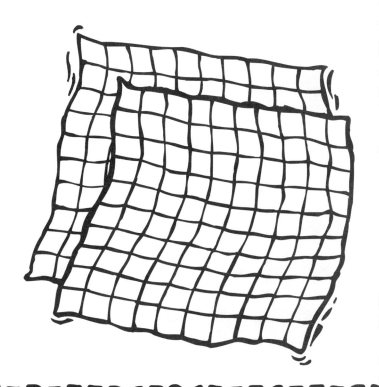

Balancing Water and Sand

For this experiment, you will need:

> a balance
> sand
> water
> *measuring spoons*
> two 8-oz. (250ml) plastic cups

Ask students which is heavier—100 teaspoons of water or 100 teaspoons of sand. After taking their guesses, put an 8-ounce paper cup on each side of the balance and pour 100 teaspoons of sand and water on each side of the balance.

Rolling Dice to 100

This game can be played by two to six players. Each person takes a turn rolling either one or two dice. The number the first person rolls is added to the number the second person rolls and so on, until the total reaches 100 exactly. As the total nears 100, the student rolling the dice may choose to throw only one die. If the total goes over 100, that roll does not count, and play continues with the next student until the number 100 is exactly reached.

100-Second Challenges

Challenge students to see how many times they can do the following activities in 100 seconds:

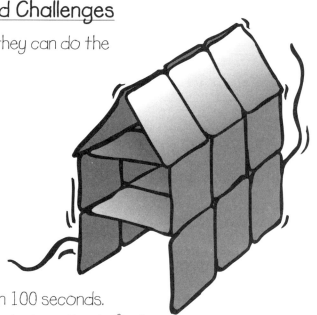

- write their names
- touch toes
- tie their shoes
- make a card house
- string beads
- connect links
- walk around the classroom
- shake hands with other students

Or, see how many words students can say in 100 seconds.
Before any of these activities, make sure students estimate first.

Spring

- Marshmallow Bunnies
- Bunny Headbands
- Hatching Chicks
- Decorating Eggs
- Easter Baskets

- Confetti Eggs
- Eggshell Mosaics
- Plastic-Egg Math
- Egg Hunt
- Eggs-periment I

- Eggs-periment II
- Viviparous or Oviparous?
- Egg Sounds Game
- Colored-Egg Twister
- Rolling Eggs Game

- Egg Relay Game
- Egg Toss
- Deviled Eggs
- Bird Nests

Marshmallow Bunnies

Spring is a time of new life. Classrooms can be decorated with pictures of baby animals and spring flowers. Make marshmallow bunnies from three large marshmallows and two toothpicks. Stick one toothpick through two marshmallows, one on top of the other. Put two half toothpicks where the ears would go, and tear off pieces from the third marshmallow to make ears. Attach candy buttons for eyes and a nose with paste made from powdered sugar and water. Caution students to remove all toothpicks before eating.

Bunny Headbands

Make a headband for each student using folded white paper. Glue cotton balls around the headband. Cut two white construction-paper ears, and two smaller pink ears. Glue the pink ears to the white ears. Cover the white part of the ears with more cotton balls, leaving the lower two inches of the ears blank. Attach the ears to the back of the headband to make fluffy bunny ears.

Hatching Chicks

Use this pattern to make a cracked egg. Students can color and cut out a little chick and glue it to the underside of the egg's bottom half. Fasten the two halves together at the side with a brad to make a chick popping out of a cracked egg.

Decorating Eggs

Decorate hard-boiled eggs the traditional way with an egg coloring kit, or try something different. Use sponges dipped in tempera paint to color the eggs. Or, make a paste out of flour and water, and paste squares of colored tissue paper around the eggs. Use several layers of tissue to make the egg darker and give it a bumpier texture.

Easter Baskets

Start collecting strawberry baskets a few weeks before the party. Students can decorate their baskets by threading ribbon or strips of paper in and out of the holes. Handles for the baskets can be made by joining two pipe cleaners and fastening each end to the basket. Tie a ribbon around the top of the handle. Finish the baskets by filling them with plastic grass or green paper strips.

Confetti Eggs

Before the party, blow out an egg for each student. Poke a 1/4" (.5cm)-diameter hole in either end of each egg with an open paper clip or needle. Blow the white and yolk out of the egg and rinse thoroughly. Give students pieces of recycled colored paper to tear into tiny pieces. Stuff the eggs with the paper and tape it closed on both sides. Send the eggs home with students so they can break them with their families.

Eggshell Mosaics

Eggshell mosaics make beautiful spring decorations. Crush eggshells from hard-boiled eggs and place them in several bowls. Sprinkle drops of food coloring to make various colors of shells. After students make a line drawing with thin black marker, have them glue the eggshell pieces in different parts of their pictures.

Plastic-Egg Math

Plastic eggs make great math manipulatives. Try estimating, counting, sorting, and graphing eggs in a basket. The eggs can be used as a nonstandard measure to check the length of various objects, such as a desk or doorway. Patterns can be made with the eggs, and the different colors can be added or subtracted. The numbers 1 through 30 can be written on the eggs, and students can put them in numerical order. Take apart some eggs and help children find congruent shapes. Students can identify ordinal positions, such as first and fifth, of eggs in a line. Coins can be put in the eggs for children to count. The eggs can also be placed in rows to introduce multiplication, or divided by the class to demonstrate division. Finally, students can think of numerous word problems to go along with the eggs.

Egg Hunt

Have a good old-fashioned egg hunt with students. Either hide eggs they've decorated in class or hide plastic eggs filled with goodies or secret messages. Make sure no egg is completely hidden. Leave a bit of each egg showing so none are left after the hunt. Put a limit on the number of eggs found per student so all students have an opportunity to find eggs. After the egg hunt is completed, count the total number of eggs found.

Eggs-periment I

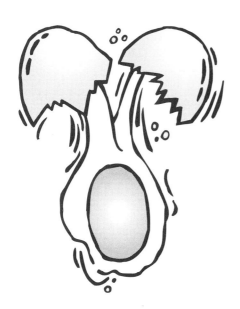

Raw or Hard Boiled?

To see if an egg is raw or hard boiled, spin both eggs. The raw egg will spin more slowly, as the yolk and white spin at a different rate than the outer shell. The hard-boiled egg spins quickly due to the solid nature of the yolk and white matching the solid outer shell.

Eggs-periment II

Can you break an egg with one bare hand?

Take an egg in one hand and squeeze it as hard as you can. The shell will not break. Be careful not to puncture the egg with your fingernail while squeezing. That will break the egg, just as a chick's egg tooth helps it break out of its shell.

Viviparous or Oviparous?

Find pictures of baby animals to sort into categories of oviparous vs. viviparous animals. Read *Chickens Aren't the Only Ones* by Ruth Heller (Grosset and Dunlap, 1981) before sorting the pictures. Oviparous animals, animals that hatch from eggs, could include birds, turtles, fish, snakes, and frogs. Viviparous animals, animals that bear live young, could include any mammal such as horses, dogs, whales, mice, tigers, and lions.

Egg Sounds Game

Play this fun, hearing game by labeling dark-colored plastic eggs from A to Z. Place small objects in pairs of eggs, including paper clips, sand, pennies, buttons, toothpicks, paper scraps, beans, corn, crayons, small blocks, raisins, cereal pieces, and feathers. Make a key that tells which eggs match. Have students sit in a circle, and give each an egg. Invite one child to shake his or her egg, and have the other students listen. Any student who thinks he or she has a matching egg stands up. The first student listens to the standing students' eggs and determines whose eggs match. Consult the key to see if students are correct.

Colored-Egg Twister

On a 50" x 70" (125cm x 175cm) section of an old white sheet or large piece of butcher paper, make a fun body twist game by coloring four rows of six different-colored eggs. Make one card for each color, and four cards labeled, *right foot*, *left foot*, *right hand* and *left hand*. Let four students play this game at a time. Place the color cards in one paper bag and the foot/hand cards in another. Choose one color card and one foot/hand card, and announce what the students are to do, such as putting the left foot on the purple egg. If a student falls, he or she is out of the game. Play continues until one students is left. Be sure to play this game on carpet or grass to cushion any falls.

Rolling Eggs Game

Be sure to use hard-boiled eggs for this fun relay game. Divide the class into two teams, and break each team into two groups. Have each group in a team line up facing the other group, with ten feet (three meters) or so in between. Give each team a hard-boiled egg to pass back and forth between groups. Students pass the eggs by rolling them across the floor with their noses. The first team to have all students pass their egg wins.

Egg Relay Game

Line up students as in the Rolling Eggs Game. Instead of rolling the eggs with their noses, students carry them under their chins without using their hands. The eggs are then passed from student to student, again without using their hands. If the eggs drop at any time, the student must return to the starting point and try again. The first team that passes the egg between all students wins.

Egg Toss

Divide the class in half and have each group stand in a line facing the other. Students standing directly across each other are partners in this fun, and potentially messy, game. Give each pair of students an egg. Make most of the eggs hard-boiled, but throw in a couple of raw ones. Have students carefully toss the eggs to each other. If a pair drops an egg, they must step out of the line. The remaining students take one step back and toss the eggs again. Tell students to be extra careful since no one knows who has the raw egg or eggs. Play continues until only one pair remains.

Deviled Eggs

Students will be pleased with this recipe they can make mostly on their own on the day before your party.

Ingredients:

6 tablespoons (90ml) mayonnaise
1 teaspoon (5ml) dry mustard
pinch of salt and pepper
12 hard boiled eggs

Materials:

fork
bowl
spoon
plastic knife
plate
plastic wrap

Peel hard-boiled eggs and cut in half lengthwise. Remove yolks and mash with fork in the bowl. Add mayonnaise, dry mustard, salt, and pepper. Place mixture by spoonful back in egg-white halves. Place on a plate, cover with plastic wrap, and refrigerate for one day before serving. Recipe makes 24 servings.

Spring

Recipe

Bird Nests

Ingredients:

2 cups (500ml) chow mein noodles

1 tablespoon (15ml) butter

1 cup (250ml) mini marshmallows

jelly-bean eggs

Materials:

electric skillet

mixing spoon

waxed paper

Heat butter and marshmallows in electric skillet. Add chow mein noodles. Let cool, and shape mixture into several tiny nests on waxed paper. Add jelly-bean eggs to make a cute and yummy bird nests. Makes 6-8 bird nests.

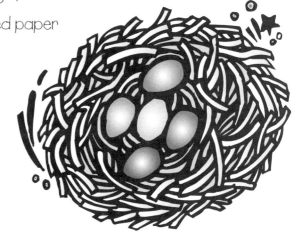

Earth Day

- Recycled Art
- Poster Campaign
- Recycled Paper Pads
- Bird Helpers

- Leaf-Rubbing Placemats
- Litter Walk
- Plant a Tree
- Calculating a Tree's Age

- Letters to the President
- Up, Rock
- Nature Memory Game

Earth Day   Arts/Crafts

Recycled Art

Treasures can be made out of trash. Start a recycling bin a week before Earth Day for items such as plastic and paper milk containers, paper cups and plates, aluminum cans, paper scraps, cracker boxes, or anything else that could be used for recycled art. Spread out all the recycled materials and let your students' creativity loose. Offer glue as the only non-recycled material for creating art. Turn your classroom into a recycled art museum, and invite other classes for a showing.

Poster Campaign

Environmental issues are brought to people's attention through promotional campaigns. Brainstorm with students how to make the Earth a better place through posters. Issues to address might include energy conservation ("Turn out the lights!"), noise pollution ("Whisper in the cafeteria."), litter ("Keep our school spotless."), or air quality ("Have you carpooled lately?"). After a certain number of days, have students take down the posters to keep them from being turned into litter.

Recycled Paper Pads

Keep a recycling box in your classroom, designed just for paper. When the box gets full, separate the paper into piles of construction paper, copy paper, and so on. Give each student a 3 1/2" x 5" (9cm x 12.5cm) sturdy pattern for cutting out pieces of paper. Put 20 pieces of paper together and put one staple in the upper left-hand corner to make a handy notepad. Jazz up the notepad by stamping a cute design in the lower right-hand corners of the papers. Sell the notepads as a fund-raiser for 25 cents each.

Bird Helpers

Instead of a bird feeder, make a bird helper to help birds make their nests. Rinse out a half-gallon (two-liter) milk carton, and cut a hole in one side toward the bottom. Put in items to help with nest-making, such as lint from a clothes dryer, string, yarn, twigs, hair from a hairbrush, small fabric scraps, or any other helpful item. Punch a hole in the top of the carton and run a string through it. Hang the bird helper on a tree near your classroom, and watch periodically for bird activity. Leave the bird helper alone for a while, and return later to see which items have been taken.

Leaf-Rubbing Placemats

Take students on a leaf walk to collect leaves for this project. Give each student some leaves; peeled green, brown and yellow crayons; and a 12" x 18" (30cm x 45cm) piece of white paper. To make a leaf rubbing, place a leaf under the paper. Using the side of a peeled crayon, color over the leaf to make an impression. Make several leaf impressions. Make a border for the placemat from these leaf patterns.

Litter Walk

Celebrate Earth Day by pitching in—pitching litter into the garbage, that is. Give each student a recycled plastic grocery bag, and take students to an area of your school campus that is in need of cleanup. Let students pick up litter, but direct them not to pick up glass, cigarette butts, or any other hazardous or germy item. Ask them beforehand to make note of the most common type of litter found, and think of ways to help stop that problem. Find a way to communicate your students' findings to other students in the school, perhaps through a poster campaign. Return on another day to see if your campaign was successful.

Plant a Tree

Earth Day is a great day to add some greenery to your school. Prior to Earth Day raise money to buy a tree by collecting cans, selling notepads made from recycled paper, or some other Earth-friendly fund-raiser. Be sure to get permission from your principal and school and district maintenance personnel. Trees are often planted in memory of some person. Think if there is anyone to whom you could dedicate your tree. If so, have a plaque made to be cemented in place near your tree.

Calculating a Tree's Age

It's hard to think of a tree as disposable when the age of that tree is revealed. Some bristlecone pines in California have been estimated to be over 4,000 years old. The age of many trees in temperate zones can be estimated by counting annual, or growth, rings. The ring is the result of differences in cell growth throughout the year. In the spring, a tree's cell growth is rapid and large. Growth of cells slows in the summer and is dormant in the winter. Growth picks up again the following spring. The change in rates of cell growth leaves a ring. It is interesting to note that scientists have observed wider rings in wet years and narrower rings in dry years. Scientists can also date certain environmental conditions to a tree's rings.

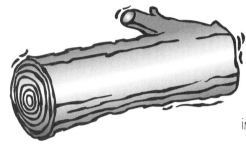

Obtain a tree-ring sample or a picture of one, and ask students to estimate the tree's age. Students can draw pictures of their own tree samples, and pass them around for other students to estimate the trees' ages. Encourage students to vary the width of the rings to correspond with imagined weather conditions.

Letters to the President

Children have strong opinions about how to make the Earth a better place. Encourage students to send their opinions to the top by having them dictate or type letters to the president. Hold a discussion beforehand on environmental issues such as air quality, recycling, and endangered animals, and list ways the president can help. The address of the White House is 1600 Pennsylvania Avenue NW, Washington, D.C. 20500. It is likely some, if not all, of your students will receive a response from the president, which is a powerful experience.

Up, Rock

Divide the class into two teams. Team A sits around a table, while Team B stands at the front of the room. Team A puts their hands under the table and begins to pass a small, flat rock from person to person. One person from Team B calls, "Up, rock," and all members hold up two fists, including the person with the rock. The Team B person then says, "Down, rock," and all Team A hands go flat on the table. The members of Team B put their heads together to decide who has the rock. If Team B guesses correctly, they get one point and take over the rock. If Team B guesses incorrectly, they lose one point. They can guess up to two more times, losing a point for each incorrect guess. If Team B makes three incorrect guesses, the game starts over with Team A passing the rock again. The winner is the first team to reach a predetermined amount of points.

Nature Memory Game

Gather 10 to 12 items from nature, such as a leaf, seed, rock, and other small objects. Arrange the objects on a large tray and cover with a towel. Give each student a pencil and piece of paper, and ask them to set their pencils down. Show them the items on the tray for 30 seconds, and cover the tray again. Ask students to write down or draw pictures of all the objects on the tray they can remember seeing. When they are finished, show the items to students again, and let them count how many they were able to remember.

Cinco de Mayo

- Group Sombreros
- Mexican Flag
- Maracas
- Coil Pots
- Numeros en Español
- De Colores
- Taco-Eating Contest
- Piñata
- Cheese Crisps

Group Sombreros

Make sombrero centerpieces for your Mexican fiesta. Give groups of three to four students a sombrero made by cutting a circle of butcher paper three feet (one meter) in diameter. Make a cone out of butcher paper to form the top of the sombrero and tape it to the circle. Give students markers, crayons, paper, glue, pom-poms and other items to decorate the sombrero. Provide pictures of sombreros for inspiration. Place the finished sombreros on desks or countertops.

Mexican Flag

The Mexican flag consists of three vertical stripes of green, white, and red, with a coat of arms in the middle. Students can make their own Mexican flags by gluing a 6" x 12" (15cm x 30cm) piece of green paper on the left side of a 12" x 18" (30cm x 45cm) piece of white construction paper. Leaving a white gap, on the far right side of the paper glue a 6" x 12" (15cm x 30cm) piece of red construction paper. Provide a picture of the Mexican flag and encourage students to copy the coat of arms.

Maracas

Collect small plastic juice bottles, paper-towel rolls, and dried beans a few weeks before your party. To make maracas with juice bottles, fill the bottle one-quarter full with beans, and tape the bottle closed. Paint the outside of the bottle with tempera. To make maracas from paper-towel rolls, cut the towel roll in half, cover one end with paper, and secure with tape. Fill the roll one-fourth full with beans, cover the other end with paper, and fasten with tape. Paint the outside with tempera. When dry, shake your creations to make a maraca sound.

Coil Pots

Coil-pot clay can be made by mixing 3 cups (375ml) flour, 1 cup (250ml) salt, 1/2 cup (125ml) vegetable oil, and 1 cup (250ml) water. Give each student a ball of clay the size of a baseball. Pull off a piece and roll out a circle 4" (10cm) in diameter. Make coil pots by rolling out clay coils 1/2" (1cm) thick and 12" (30cm) long. Layer coils one on top of another. Let the clay dry for this special Cinco de Mayo fiesta souvenir. Makes 8 coil pots.

Numeros en Espanol

Teach children the numbers one through ten, or 12 through 20 if your students already can count to ten in Spanish.

1 - uno (oo-noe)
2 - dos (dōs)
3 - tres (tray-es)
4 - cuatro (kwa-troe)
5 - cinco (seen-koe)
6 - seis (say-es)
7 - siete (see-e-tay)

8 - ocho (oe-choe)
9 - nueve (noo-e-vay)
10 - diez (dee-ay-es)
11 - once (oen-say)
12 - doce (doe-say)
13 - trece (tray-say)
14 - catorce (ka-tor-say)

15 - quince (keen-say)
16 - dieciseis (dee-ay-es-ee-say-es)
17 - diecisiete (dee-ay-es-ee-see-e-tay)
18 - dieciocho (dee-ay-es-ee-oe-choe)
19 - diecinueve (dee-ay-es-ee-noo-e vay)
20 - veinte (vayn-tay)

Instead of playing "Mother May I?," play a game of "Señora (or Señor) May I?" Have students stand in a line. Then say to one student, "You may take cuatro (or some other number) steps." If this is the first time saying numbers in Spanish, you may need to help students figure out what the number means. The student then says, "Señora (or Señor), may I?" You reply, "Yes, you may," and he or she takes that many steps closer to you. If the student forgets to say "Señora, may I?," he or she loses a turn, and play continues with the next student. The winner is the student who reaches you first.

De Colores

Teach students colors in Spanish.

red - rojo (roe-hoe)   blue - azul (a-sool)

green - verde (vayr-day)   yellow - amarillo (o-mo-ree-yoe)

orange - anaranjado (o-nu-ron-ho-doe)   purple - morado (moe-ro-doe)

black - negro (ne-groe)   white - blanco (blon-koe)

Sing this color song to the tune of "Row, Row, Row Your Boat:"

Teacher sings: *De colores, de colores, Are you wearing rojo?*

Students wearing red stand and sing: *I am wearing rojo, si, I am wearing rojo!* Those students then sit and another color is called.

Cinco de Mayo   Game

Taco-Eating Contest

Serve tacos at your fiesta, and make a game out of eating them! Give each child who wishes to participate a taco to be eaten over a paper plate. The object of the game is to eat the taco without spilling. Fill the taco with lots of lettuce for an added challenge. If anything spills out, it must stay on the plate. The winner is the student with the least amount of taco droppings on his or her plate.

Piñata

What would a fiesta be without a piñata? Piñata breaking, however, can lead to fights over candy. Avert this problem by showing a poster of the candy to be collected, and turn piñata-breaking into a scavenger hunt. When stuffing the piñata, use five different kinds of candy, putting in enough for each child to have one of all kinds, plus some extra. Make a poster displaying the five kinds of candy, and challenge children to find one of each. When students find all five kinds, they can step away from the area and let other students find their candy.

Cinco de Mayo

Recipe

Cheese Crisps

Ingredients:
(for each child)
   1 soft tortilla
   1/4 cup (63ml) shredded cheddar cheese

Materials:
   cheese grater
   cookie tray

Cheese crisps are Mexican food favorites for most kids, and they're easy to make. Students can even shred the cheese using a cheese grater under adult supervision. Sprinkle a soft tortilla with the shredded cheese , and place under a broiler until the cheese melts.

Mother's Day

- Mother's Day Tea
- Personalized Stationery
- Potholders
- Pressed Flowers

- Refrigerator Magnets
- Mother's Day Play
- Acrostic Poem

- Songfest
- That's My Mom!
- Finger Sandwiches

Mother's Day   Decorations

Mother's Day Tea

Have a Mother's Day Tea, and invite students' mothers to attend. Send home student-designed invitations at least three weeks in advance so that working moms can make arrangements to attend. Invite grandmothers, aunts, and other special women in cases where mothers cannot attend. Decorate your room with plastic and real plants. Students can make bud vases ahead of time by taking a 7" (17.5cm) piece of PVC pipe, approximately 5/8" (2cm) in diameter, which can be found in most hardware stores. Place the pipe in a ball of Plaster of Paris or hardening clay, and shape the ball like the bottom of a bud vase. Let dry, and then cover with squares of colored tissue paper and paste made from flour and water. Layer until the pipe and ball are no longer visible. Let dry. Write the student's name and year on the bottom of the vase, and place one plastic or real flower inside.

Personalized Stationery

Mothers will treasure a gift of personalized stationery. Give each student five 8 1/2" x 11" (21cm x 27.5cm) and five 5 1/2" x 8 1/2" (14cm x 21cm) pieces of white, pink, or yellow copy paper. Show students how to make a monogram with the first initial of their mother's last name. Or, students can decorate the upper left-hand corner of each piece of stationery with flowers and another appropriate picture or design. Ink stamps and stickers can be used as well. Another way to make stationery is with catchy slogans across the top, such as *I'm the Mother, Queen Mother,* or some other idea students create.

Potholders

Plain potholders can be purchased at craft supply stores and decorated with tempera paint. Either go with a simple handprint, or give students small brushes and several colors of paint to make more detailed designs. A thin permanent marker can be used to write students' names and the year on the potholders.

Pressed Flowers

This art project can be completed before or during the Mother's Day party, but the flowers must be pressed beforehand. About a week prior, have students collect four to six flowers each to press in between the pages of a book. Take dried, pressed flowers and glue them to a 6" x 9" (15cm x 22.5cm) piece of construction paper. Cover the flowers with wide transparent packing tape, contact paper, or plastic wrap. Frame the "pictures" with cutout paper flowers.

Refrigerator Magnets

Refrigerator magnets are easier than ever to make, thanks to magnetic tape available in most craft, teacher supply, and some grocery stores. Attach a photo of each student to a pink or red heart shape. Have the student write *Happy Mother's Day*, or *I love you, Mom*, and his or her name and the date on the heart. Glitter, sequins, and other craft materials can be added to jazz up the heart. Place magnetic tape on the back of each heart as is, or laminate the hearts before adding the magnet.

Mother's Day Play

Choose a special story for your students to act out for their mothers. Good choices include *Are You My Mother?* by P.D. Eastman (Beginner Books, 1960) and *Love You, Forever* by Robert Munsch (Firefly Books, 1986). *Are You My Mother?* offers many roles for students, and simple costumes can be made by wearing a poster of the character being played. *Love You, Forever* includes for fewer parts, but the lines can be read by different students. Students can sing the repetitive song together. There won't be a dry eye in the classroom.

Acrostic Poem

A few days before the party, create an acrostic poem with the class. Write the letters of the word *Mother* on a large piece of chart paper. Ask students to think of words that describe mothers to correspond with each letter. For example, "M is for magnificent," and "O is for often gives hugs." Make a class acrostic poem and let the students read it to their mothers. Have students take turns reading the lines of the poem in fours or fives, giving all children a chance to participate.

Songfest

Treat students' mothers to a songfest. Begin practicing several weeks beforehand. Songs about love and caring are good choices, as well as any classroom favorites you've been singing together throughout the year. You may even wish to take requests. About 10 to 15 minutes of songs is ideal for a party setting.

That's My Mom!

Ask the following questions about students' moms. If question relates to a student's mom, that student shouts out, "That's my mom!"

Whose mom . . .

loves to read?
cries at sad movies?
says, "because I said so!"?
smells pretty?
drives a motorcycle?
wears glasses?
cooks great food?
mows the lawn?
wakes up early?

(cont'd)

That's My Mom! – continued

uses a computer?

has a funny laugh?

gives great hugs?

sings?

plays a musical instrument?

works outside the home?

drives a fast car?

kisses boo-boos?

fixes things well?

is your mom? (All students point to their moms, and this question ends the game.)

Think of other questions tailored to your students' moms.

Finger Sandwiches

Along with tea, serve student-made finger sandwiches! Give each student two slices of white or whole-wheat bread, and invite them to cut identical shapes out of each piece. Students can spread plain or strawberry cream cheese on one shape and cover with the other piece. Or, cut circles of bread about 2" (5cm) in diameter. Spread cream cheese over the circle and top with a cucumber slice.

Father's Day

- "I Love My Dad" Pancakes
- Dad Notepads
- Funny Tie Contest
- Tie Cards
- You'll Never Believe
  What My Dad Did!
- Pancake Breakfast

"I Love My Dad" Pancakes

Have a pancake breakfast with students' fathers before school one day. Give each child a tan piece of paper in the shape of a pancake, and have him or her finish the sentence *I love my dad because . . .* on the "pancake." Put the pancakes on paper plates. Cut little squares of "butter" from yellow paper and write students' names on the squares. Glue a square to each pancake without covering any of the words. The pancakes can be displayed individually on plates, or placed in stacks on several plates to be delivered during the breakfast.

I Love my dad because Sara

Dad Notepads

Give each child ten pieces of 4" x 6" (10cm x 15cm) white paper to make a notepad for dad. On each piece, the student can write a phrase such as, *My dad's the best!* or *I have one bad dad!* Staple the papers in the upper left-hand corner. Note papers can also be decorated with stickers or ink stamps. Students can wrap the notepads and give them to their dads at the pancake breakfast.

Funny Tie Contest

Encourage dads to wear their funniest or strangest ties to the Father's Day breakfast, even if they are not wearing a suit (which can be even funnier). Let each dad stand up and show his tie, and use a clap-meter method for determining which tie is funniest. Tell students they must clap for all dads' ties. But, if a tie is especially funny, they can clap louder. Listen for the top three to five ties on the clap meter, and hold a vote between those ties to see which dad has the funniest tie. Give the winning dad a tie-shaped award.

Tie Cards

Give each student a piece of paper in the shape of a tie for making unique Father's Day cards. Have them paint the ties with watercolor or tempera paint, encouraging them to recall a tie they have seen their dad wear. Have students write the card messages on separate pieces of paper, and glue to the painted ties when dry.

Father's Day

Game

You'll Never Believe What My Dad Did!

Some dads have done amazing things. Have each dad write on a sentence strip one interesting thing he has done in his lifetime, such as jumping out of an airplane or putting together a 1,000-piece puzzle. The event need not be fantastic, as kids are impressed with even small things their dads have done.

Pull each sentence strip out of a hat and read it aloud to the class. Invite students to guess which dad did each amazing thing.

Pancake Breakfast

Use this recipe to make pancakes with dads. For one batch, you will need:

Ingredients:

3 cups (750ml) flour

4 tablespoons (60ml) sugar

4 teaspoons (20ml) baking powder

1 teaspoon (5ml) salt

2 eggs

2 cups (500ml) milk

2 teaspoons (10ml) cooking oil

applesauce or syrup

Materials:

large mixing bowl

small mixing bowl

wire whisk

fork

spatula

electric skillet

measuring spoons

measuring cups

(cont'd)

Pancake Breakfast - continued

Put the flour, sugar, baking powder, and salt in the large mixing bowl and set aside. Beat the eggs with a fork in the small bowl and add milk. Pour the smaller bowl's ingredients into the larger bowl, and blend with a wire whisk until smooth, although some lumps may remain. Put cooking oil in the electric skillet and heat. Drop the batter by tablespoons to make silver dollar pancakes, which will go further than full-sized pancakes. Give each dad an opportunity to be the "flipper." Serve pancakes with syrup and/or applesauce.

End of the School Year

- Sandscapes
- "End of School Year" Books
- Special Awards
- Summer Olympics

- Water Relay
- Ready, Aim, Squirt
- Water Balloon Toss

Sandscapes

Summertime is fun time, and for some students that means trips to the beach or a lake. Invite the class to make sandscapes for summertime party decorations. To make a sandscape, fill a Styrofoam or plastic plate with moist sand. Smooth with a plastic fork. Decorate the sandscape with shells, rocks, twigs, leaves, tiny umbrellas, and any other small object to make a beach or lakefront scene.

"End of School Year" Books

Start making books for students about a month before the end of school. Include items such as favorite songs, poems, and recipes from the school year. Copy some photos taken over the year and place them throughout the books. Think of high points of the school year, and list them on a page entitled *Remember When?* Include an end-of-the-school-year letter to your students, encouraging them to read over the summer and visit you next year. Leave the last three pages blank for students to gather autographs from classmates on the last day.

Special Awards

Recognize students' special talents with end-of-the-year awards. Some award ideas include:

Smile Award	Bookworm Award	Class Comedian Award
Sports Award	Friendship Award	Peacemaker Award
Singing Award	Best Builder Award	Math Whiz Award
Helper Award	Computer Pro Award	Super Rope Jumper Award
Collector Award	Junior Scientist Award	Animal Lover Award
Artistic Award	Puzzle-making Award	Dancing Award
Leggomaniac Award	Handwriting Award	Super Speller Award

Make up other awards to fit your students. Be sure that all students receive an award. Give the awards out in front of the whole class, and invite students to clap and cheer for each other.

Summer Olympics

Here's a helpful list of activities for a fun-for-all End of the School Year Party. These activities could be used in either competitive or cooperative settings, one-on-one or group contests, an "adventure" course, supervised stations, or large-group activities.

Running	Pushing	Stacking/Knocking Down
Jumping	Pulling	Arranging
Skipping	Hopping	Hiding/Seeking
Sliding	Hula-Hooping	Collecting
Balancing	Jumping Rope	Digging
Crawling	Throwing/Tossing	Climbing
Swinging	Catching	Splashing
Rolling	Building	

Water Relay

Gather four large buckets, and fill two of them with an equal amount of water. Divide class into two teams, and have each team line up behind a bucket filled with water. Place the empty buckets across from the filled ones approximately 20 feet (7 meters) away. The first person in each line takes a cup, fills it with water from the bucket, and pours the water into the empty bucket across from his or her team. If any water is spilled, that person must start again. The runner returns and hands the empty cup to the next person in line. Allow teams to continue for a set amount of time, long enough for each person to have a turn, but not so long that the bucket is emptied. Blow a whistle when time is up, and measure how much water is in each bucket. The winning team will have the highest water level in the far bucket.

Ready, Aim, Squirt!

Water is a great medium for outside end-of-the school-year games. Set out two empty plastic soda bottles and place a Ping-Pong ball on each. Give two students matching water guns or spray bottles filled with water, and stand them a distance away from the soda bottles. Challenge the students to knock off the Ping-Pong ball by squirting it with water. The first student to knock off the ball wins, and two more students take their places. The distance the students stand away from the soda bottle will depend on the strength of the water guns or squirt bottles. Determine beforehand a challenging distance for this game.

Water Balloon Toss

Balloons designed specifically to be filled with water are available at most grocery and toy stores. Fill up enough balloons for students to have at least two tries with this game. Divide the class in half and have each group stand in a line facing the other. Students standing directly across are partners in this fun and potentially wet game. Give each pair of students a water balloon. Have partners toss the water balloons to each other. If a pair breaks their water balloon, they *must* step out of the line. The remaining students take one step back and toss the balloons again. Play continues until only one pair remains.

Reproducible